5-15-70

THE NONPROFESSIONAL
REVOLUTION IN
MENTAL HEALTH

THE NONPROFESSIONAL REVOLUTION IN MENTAL HEALTH

FRANCINE SOBEY

COLUMBIA UNIVERSITY PRESS

NEW YORK AND LONDON

1970

FOREWORD

1536251

Salvador Minuchin, in an editorial in the *American Journal of Orthopsychiatry*, states that ". . . . the inclusion of paraprofessionals in the existing structures of delivery of service brought to a head a bipolarity of approaches to mental illness which was already incipient in the field."* The bipolarity refers to the activist sociological emphasis on the one hand and the more traditional internally oriented approach on the other. But the significant point is that of the role ascribed to the paraprofessional as a strategic catalyst in the field of mental health. It is in this context that Francine Sobey's extremely relevant book, *The Nonprofessional Revolution in Mental Health*, should be viewed.

The book is crucial for anyone concerned with the major adjustments which must take place in the mental health field so that large numbers of people in need may be served adequately. It is based on a study of over 10,000 nonprofessionals

---

* Salvador Minuchin, "The Paraprofessional and the Use of Confrontation in the Mental Health Field," *The American Journal of Orthopsychiatry*, October 1969, p. 724.

working in 185 National Institute of Mental Health sponsored projects across the country.

The findings are striking indeed. Nonprofessionals are utilized not simply because professional manpower is unavailable but rather to provide new services in innovative ways. Nonprofessionals are providing such therapeutic functions as individual counseling, group counseling, activity group therapy, milieu therapy; they are doing case finding; they are playing screening roles of a nonclerical nature; they are helping people to adjust to community life; they are providing special skills such as tutoring; they are promoting client self-help through involving clients in helping others having similar problems.

It is noteworthy that their main function has not been to relieve professional staff of tasks requiring less than professional expertise. The major finding is that nonprofessionals are being trained for new service functions and roles, in many cases roles that were not previously being played at all in the mental health program.

Although the research does not allow easily for evaluating the effectiveness of the nonprofessional in reducing mental illness or improving mental health, Professor Sobey finds strong indirect support from the professionals who were interviewed. The book reports that "overwhelmingly the project directors in the NIMH projects felt that the service performed by nonprofessionals justified the expense of training, supervision and general agency overhead." This is an area of increasing concern as the human services move toward greater accountability, and there is a growing literature on the role that nonprofessionals play in improving human services.*

---

* See Alan Gartner, "Do Paraprofessionals Improve Human Services: First Critical Appraisal of the Data," New Careers Development Center, June 1969.

Dr. Sobey points out the special value of teaming of the professional and nonprofessional in producing an improved quality and quantity of output in the mental health field. The team concept has added support from Neugeboren's study of the New Haven poverty program, where it was found that the combination of professional and paraprofessional in a social service team provides the most effective kind of service. The New Haven study found that given the same number of contacts with clients, teams consisting of a professional social worker and either a paraprofessional homemaker adviser or neighborhood worker were more successful in solving clients' problems than a team of professionals or paraprofessionals alone. Such teams achieved positive results with fewer contacts than social workers operating independently.

The importance of this book is that it does not simply argue for the extended use of nonprofessionals on the basis of manpower shortages, which of course are self-evident in the mental health and human service fields; rather it makes its case largely in terms of the need for expanded service and preventive mental health care.

February, 1970   Frank Riessman

ACKNOWLEDGMENTS

Many persons and agencies have contributed to the content of this book, and I am pleased to acknowledge their assistance. In the writing of several chapters I have drawn upon research performed and funded under Contract No. PH 43-66-967 with the National Institute of Mental Health. Public Health Service, Department of Health, Education and Welfare. To Mrs. Ruth Knee, Chief of the Mental Health Care Administration of NIMH, I am indebted for helpful liaison with NIMH during my direction of the research program on nonprofessional utilization at the Center of Research and Demonstration, Columbia University School of Social Work. Samuel Finestone, Dean of the Center for Research and Demonstration, gave his time and expertise unsparingly from the earliest conceptualizations to the final evaluation of the research. Others at Columbia University who contributed to the research were Mrs. Beatrice Mittelman, Programming Supervisor at the Computer Center, Teacher's College, Professor I. Lukoff, Doran Teague, Yetta Appel, Sofie Theobald, Barbara Golden, and Gloria Abate, a volunteer, now teaching at the University of Lima in Peru. Dana Mooring gave valuable advice on organizing the manuscript from voluminous research findings and my own mental health field experience. At Columbia University Press, John D. Moore and Frederick

Nicklaus helped considerably with their astute suggestions and valuable editorial services.

To all of the above, but especially to the anonymous "non-professionals" and the project directors whose work and ideas created the interest to write this book, I am most indebted. I wish to thank, too, the many faculty colleagues at Columbia and other universities who urged me to write this book for use as a text for students and teachers at community colleges, colleges, graduate and professional schools, and for the concerned citizen in community education programs. To my family, too, for their flexibility in assuming many "new" roles in order to permit the completion of this manuscript, warmest thanks.

None of the above-mentioned is responsible for opinions, evaluations, and interpretations made in this manuscript.

Francine Sobey
Professor of Social Work
Columbia University

New York City
March 1969

CONTENTS

Foreword

Acknowledgments

1 Manpower Implications of the Mental Health Crisis   1

2 Concepts and Trends in Manpower Utilization   16

3 The Nature of Mental Health Programs   44

4 Characteristics of the Nonprofessional Population   73

5 Functions Performed by Nonprofessional and Professional Staff   97

6 Recruitment, Training, and Supervision of Nonprofessionals   109

7 Research Findings in Prevention and Innovation   122

8 Evaluation of Nonprofessionals   150

CONTENTS

9   Implications for the Seventies   176

     Appendix A: Questionnaire Used in the Survey   195

     Appendix B: Instructions to Scorers of Individual
                 Questionnaires   213

     Selected Bibliography   219

     Index   233

THE NONPROFESSIONAL
REVOLUTION IN
MENTAL HEALTH

1

MANPOWER IMPLICATIONS OF
THE MENTAL HEALTH
CRISIS

INTRODUCTION

This book is rooted in a crisis. An estimated nineteen million Americans suffer from mental illness. Five million alcoholics need treatment. Accurate figures on drug addiction are difficult to obtain, but reports from high schools and colleges indicate a steady increase in the use of drugs among the youth of the nation. The fear of violent crimes against public figures and the average citizen is now extreme. Youth account for a consistently increasing percentage of crime, greater even than their increasing percentage of the population. Many of the aged, living longer than their forebears, appear desolate and without a sense of human worth. For many Americans, the problems of mental illness are compounded by poverty, social inequality, and a grim, urban environment.

For the average citizen in the nation's cities, new crises are created daily by the maddening complexity of coping with the growing, impersonal bureaucracies, through which vital information and services are processed. A critical period in race relations has arrived. Family agencies report increasing numbers of separated and divorced parents who are seeking help with the special difficulties of child-rearing in the one-parent family. In a fast-moving, technologically-based society, the lack of consistent, maternal care in infancy and of a stable relationship with at least one parent during youth augments a growing sense of rootlessness and alienation which characterizes people's lives in this era. We now possess understanding and techniques to treat problems tied to instinctual repression (thanks to the genius of Sigmund Freud). But a new urgency compels us to comprehend and prevent the sporadic acting-out of destructive impulses, symptomatic of the succession of crises which have become chronic in this anomic era. The life, the values, the surface behavior of people is rapidly changing, but emotional needs, and the capacity to adapt to social change, by comparison move at a snail's pace.

Clearly, the solution to the problem is not limited to treating any number of psychiatric patients in the nation's hospitals and clinics, but includes diminishing emotional hazards in the home and out in the community. The potential for health in those who are already sick must be increased so that they can return to their communities, but the sickness potential in the average citizen must be decreased too. We are all vulnerable to stress, and, for some groups in society, life has offered little opportunity to build resistance to stress. Creating an environment more conducive to mental health demands more than the birth of a new genius to light the way for us. In striving for shared goals, massive human energies, properly directed, are required.

First we must face some hard facts. Supply of professionals to treat the mentally ill lags seriously behind demand. The outlook for substantially increasing the supply of professionals in the core disciplines (psychiatrists, social workers, nurses, psychologists) is doubtful indeed. Meanwhile, the demand for treatment grows as the population increases. The demand for facilities has also increased through hospital insurance coverage for psychiatric illness, labor union mental health care plans, Medicare, neighborhood public mental health centers, and other expanding programs which promise to their audience not only psychiatric treatment, but also counseling, vocational guidance, and the whole range of newer mental health services.

The chemotherapy revolution has changed the lot of mental hospital patients. No longer doomed to years of vegetation and catatonic stupor, the average patient becomes accessible to psychotherapy and the social therapies following modern drug therapy. But who will give the psychotherapy and the social rehabilitation for which the mentally ill are ready? The American public has no choice, if it wants to care for the untreated mentally ill, but to consider alternatives to personal care for every sick person by a trained psychiatrist.

Although core professionals will continue in short supply, there were six times as many nonprofessionals and new professional helpers to M.D.s in 1960 as there were in 1900;[1] current estimates are that the ratio is rapidly rising, and that nonprofessionals, in particular, will become more numerous compared with all professionals in mental health. Yet, numbers alone will not solve a single mental health problem. Is it not possible that the goal of social rehabilitation of the mentally ill can be accomplished more successfully and less expensively with the use of nonprofessional resources? A more comprehensive, coordinated approach to improving the mental health of the average citizen

---

[1] George James, Dean of Mount Sinai School of Medicine, in speech entitled "New Developments in Evaluation and Selection of Health Personnel," Annual Meeting of the American Public Health Association, San Francisco, Nov. 4, 1966.

suggests that we allocate funds and manpower resources to activities calculated to prevent the mental health crises with which we are plagued. If we know ways of preventing family breakdown, for example, how can we condone using our funds merely to aid members of disintegrated families to deal with the effects of separation through foster home care for the children, and separate living arrangements for parents? And how could we possibly plan for a wide range of preventive mental health services—educational, counseling, reaching-out, and expediting social services—without drawing upon new manpower resources?

We suspect that there is waste and under-utilization of the existing scarce professional mental health manpower. We know that we have hardly begun to tap the manpower potential in the young, the aged, housewives, and whole groups of minorities for service in mental health. The need is to optimize the use of available professionals and to study the potential of the new nonprofessional manpower (paid and volunteer) for the prevention and treatment of mental illness in this country.

The extent to which some have already undertaken this task is encouraging. Ways have been suggested of moving further along the road to alleviate the complex mental health crisis, and to improve the lot of vulnerable groups—the young and the old, the poor, and the oppressed minorities. Crisis offers opportunity as well as danger. Some of us are learning to help ourselves, while we help others and our communities, to emerge from crisis strengthened, functioning at a higher level than before.

THE PERSPECTIVE OF THE BOOK

Despite the decided consensus that there exists a critical shortage of professional mental health manpower which can not be alleviated in this period of rapid population growth and social change, little systematic research on the extent and nature of alternative forms of manpower utilization has been done. Periodically, public figures express the urgent need to tap new sources of manpower. A few individual demonstration projects have been highly publicized. The "new nonprofessional" and the indigenous nonprofessional in a very few agency settings have been described and romanticized. Dramatic reports of these in the mass media concern only a handful of experimental approaches, principally in New York City or Washington, D.C. Efforts are being made by Frank Reissman and others to launch large-scale programs of jobs with career ladders in health, education and welfare for nonprofessionals, with evaluation and research as a part of them.

But the overall view of the nature and the extent of nonprofessional utilization throughout the United States is remarkably spotty. The simplest descriptive facts of how many paid and volunteer nonprofessionals work in mental health and what they do are unknown.[2] Research efforts are fragmented, and uncoordinated. For rational practical planning at all levels, in both governmental and nongovernmental agencies, concrete, comprehensive information about nonprofessional usage is needed.

This book offers a study of nonprofessionals working to help people with problems in mental health. It describes the programs in which they are employed, the objectives of those programs, and the professionals who work with them to provide care for specified groups of people.

Who the nonprofessionals are, what they do, how they are

_____

[2] As recently as May 1969, this dearth of basic survey data on nonprofessionals was documented in *Allied Health Manpower: Trends and Prospects* by Harry Greenfield, Columbia University Press, 1969, pp. 188-89.

recruited, trained, and evaluated by their project directors will be presented here. The consequences to the mental health field of using nonprofessionally trained persons are reflected upon, and models for their future use are suggested.

Yet, something more than description of nonprofessionals and their tasks is urgently needed to deepen our understanding of manpower problems in the mental health field. More is at issue than critically scarce manpower resources in mental health. In time, the continuous cry for more manpower is destined to be heeded less and less if people resign themselves to the seeming hopelessness of the problem, and cease to wonder about how we can attack mental health problems at their source.

Manpower for what? Is it to ease, in some small, albeit necessary, manner the suffering of any number of people who break down predictably year after year? Or, is it to search for the many sources of these problems with the hope that if we learn to stem the tide of mental and social disorder, much less manpower will eventually be required to care for already disturbed persons?

Exactly where are our energies going in the mental health field? To treat those already seriously and chronically disordered (defined as tertiary prevention in this inquiry)? To identify those children and adults who show beginning signs of disturbance for which prompt diagnosis and effective treatment might ward off more serious disorders (labeled secondary prevention)?[3] Or, to provide health-promoting services for the general

---

[3] An important example of secondary prevention is suggested in the report of the National Commission on the Causes and Prevention of Violence, submitted to President Johnson on Jan. 9, 1969. The report indicated that the key to violence in American society seems to lie with the young, possibly with a relatively small number of them, whose identity science may be able to establish early for purposes of preventive action (*The New York Times,* Jan. 31, 1969).

public (for example, improved mental health education, housing, homemaker care, day care, and financial aid) and specific protective activities such as counseling during expected periods of stress for the general public—all of which are calculated to reduce the incidence of mental and social disorders (defined as primary prevention)?

If there has been little research on the extent and nature of alternative forms of manpower utilization, still less is available on the subject of levels of preventive intervention in this rapidly changing mental health field. How then can we understand what nonprofessionals are actually doing at all levels of prevention and rehabilitation?

Gerald Caplan, in *Principles of Preventive Psychiatry*, laments that although some professionals perceive the importance of beginning to work to promote mental health, and to thereby prevent the onset of mental illness, there has been little study of mental health as opposed to mental illness, and the specific nature and levels of preventive efforts needed for the general public. Without explicit recognition of what is meant by "prevention," it has been impossible to communicate about comparable experience and to advance the discipline of preventive mental health. This lack of a clear definition among professionals does not help in planning for new manpower usage. If we anticipate that greater use of nonprofessionals will have to be made in the future to promote community mental health and to prevent mental illness, we will first have to better understand and communicate what we mean by the whole continuum of prevention and its relationship to treatment and rehabilitation.

To begin to guide mental health planners in the formulation of manpower policy in this field, a meaningful conceptual framework is required. The public health classification of preventive levels as primary, secondary, and tertiary was developed for use in the research on which this book was based; that is, mental health programs were described as operating mainly on at least one of these levels. Since the data lent themselves naturally to this classification system, this framework was used to enrich our understanding of nonprofessional roles at all interventive levels. In other words, in addition to the concrete objectives of this book, the author wishes to contribute knowledge about the entire mental health field with its rapidly changing interventive systems.

This book attempts to reveal whether we have, in fact, moved beyond the confines of the traditional medical model with its emphasis on the relatively closed doctor-patient system to a broad-based public health intervention system for the entire community.

This broad interventive framework, which encompasses all three levels of mental health and disorder, presents a public health approach to be implemented by comprehensive community plans which include prevention, treatment, and rehabilitation of mental disorders, and which are coordinated with other community programs in health, education, and welfare.

In this vastly broadened field of operations, it seems likely that eventually the human relationship and educational aspects of the helping process will predominate over the traditional medical and psychiatric knowledge usually needed for the clinically diagnosed "patient." Greater use could be made of nonprofessional staff along the whole continuum of prevention and rehabilitation.

Some key findings concerning the nature of preventive efforts are presented in this book in order to clarify the nebulous concept of "prevention." Chapter 7, entitled "Research Findings in Prevention and Innovation," is directed to the serious student who is interested in the detailed, step-by-step process of learn-

8

ing to apply the conceptual framework of the book. It is particularly geared to those who desire a path for planning further research in prevention. The author's hope is that if planners learn where we are in fact failing to place our energies in mental health programs, they will wish to correct the imbalanced emphasis on gross pathology and therapeutic activities as compared with preventive efforts directed toward a wider public.

In past centuries, mental illness was considered to be strictly physiological, and the mentally deranged, the handicapped, and the needy were thrown together in asylums to protect the community from witnessing their hardship and their wrath. Although more humane attitudes toward the mentally ill developed, and the need for scientific treatment became accepted, the many-factored causes of illness were ignored by all except for a few far-seeing leaders who exhorted the public, but to little avail. Community funds were allocated to the treatment of the major mental illnesses, but practically no funds could be raised for scientific prevention. Even as late as 1961 the Joint Commission on Mental Illness and Health urged Congress to concentrate on the treatment of the mentally ill, and to delay emphasis on preventive measures in mental health.

Presumed manpower shortages should not retard a rationally conceived preventive program with focus on total communities and certain populations within these communities. There are encouraging signs that new manpower sources may have much to offer the community in preventive roles. The neighborhood planned parenthood aide who helps an overburdened mother learn how to limit her family so that she can better care for the children she already has, the teacher-mom who offers encouragement and attention so that a deprived child wants to learn— these and other nonprofessionals to be described suggest that a few of us have already begun to work directly with people before they become ill or maladapted.

If planned parenthood aides and elementary school tutors are examples of preventive mental health personnel, is *any* sort of assistance to people with problems *not* now included under the aegis of mental health? The answer is that the planning base for mental health operations has shifted from individual diagnostic case-study to epidemiological research. As a result, new services—large-scale saturation programs of preschool check-ups, services to teenaged unmarried mothers, school dropouts, etc.— are being offered for the first time in some areas of the country.

When community leaders in Woodlawn Illinois were asked recently to help establish priorities in developing a community mental health center there, they expressed their primary interest in "prevention" programs which would help make mental health principles better understood by teachers, policemen, ministers, and other key persons in the community, as well as in working directly with people before they became ill or maladapted. It is hoped that viable mental health principles will become so well understood and integrated into the work of key community personnel that these principles will no longer be considered the province of mental health professionals.

INNOVATIONS IN MANPOWER USAGE

Both new and traditional uses of nonprofessional manpower in mental health will be presented in this book, because no source of personnel should be overlooked when needs are both sizeable and urgent. Innovations in the use of nonprofessionals for a wide range of mental health functions are needed not only to compensate for the present lack of trained mental health professionals in the country, but also to experiment with the new models of comprehensive community mental health care, encouraged by such legislation as the Federal Community Mental Health Centers Act of 1963. Furthermore, in the interest of the income-seeking nonprofessional, employment in the human serv ices field (which is not likely to become as automated as commerce and industry) has much to offer potential manpower groups—housewives, retired persons, high school dropouts, college students, and particularly those in minority and under-privileged groups.

Although nonprofessionals were first considered chiefly as an expedient resource in providing custodial care for the mentally ill or charity for the poor, now they are carving out other roles for themselves, roles which some believe they can fulfill better than professionals because of their special characteristics and attributes.

In the context of this focus on "innovation," and special or "unique" roles, a caveat is in order. Very few ideas and actions are truly "new," "innovative," or "unique," especially when viewed historically. The "new" foster care and home care programs for the mentally ill, which will be discussed, were utilized in Belgium in the 1500s. We will interpret innovation pragmatically as "first time use" in a particular agency in a particular locale of this country. A home care program using psychiatric aides for the first time in home treatment of the mentally ill in a small town in Iowa, is, for the purposes of this inquiry, an "innovation" in manpower usage. There are, indeed, some "first time" programs in particular agencies which are relatively new in the entire field. Also there are some "first time" roles—such as those of indigenous mental health counselors and expeditors—for persons with little formal schooling. Greater use of "new" nonprofessionals with all levels of training (rather than sole concentration on the few able to achieve professional training)

11

should be considered as a prime solution to mental health manpower problems.

But first, what is meant by a nonprofessional? The term does not appear in the dictionaries. Sometimes referred to as auxiliary, ancillary, paraprofessional, or subprofessional, the term nonprofessional tells us only that the person is *not* a professional, that is, that he has not completed the customary formal training in any of the professional disciplines. But what is he, and what does he do? For our purposes, a nonprofessional is a paid or unpaid person (without the above-mentioned training) who works directly with individuals or community groups in providing mental health services to the public.[4] Some volunteers are professionals in other fields (for example, lawyers, clergymen). Here we call them volunteer nonprofessionals in view of their lack of professional mental health training. Volunteers are further defined as persons who offer services without fixed remuneration, either in the form of salaries or stipends.

The term "mental health" is perhaps more confusing than "nonprofessional." To deal with the broad dimensions of the mental health crisis, the term "mental health" is insufficient. Mental health involves not only the health of the mind, but also the social and ecological environment. Obviously, even an abundance of mental-health professionals and nonprofessionals alone would not be able to abate the "mental health" crisis. Many others—urban planners, social scientists, philosophers, humanists, politicians—need to collaborate with mental health ex-

---

[4] Meaning of *direct* work was given in the Instructions Manual which accompanied the questionnaire which was developed by the author to learn about nonprofessional usage. (See Appendix A for questionnaire) Working *directly* was interpreted to mean face-to-face and collateral contacts to provide a mental health service to individual patients, clients, their families, and community members. It excluded activities which were primarily clerical, administrative, research, or maintenance.

perts to decide what goals we should pursue in mental health. Yet, even then it will be up to the next generation to decide how many of these goals they will accept in planning for the mental health of their children.

SOURCES OF INFORMATION

The major tools for this book, in addition to the author's therapeutic, research, and social work experience in the mental health field since 1946, are the author's continuing inquiry into the concepts of preventive intervention in mental health, and research data collected and analyzed from 1966 to 1968 under National Institute of Mental Health sponsorship. This book presents the findings of a survey of 185 National Institute of Mental Health sponsored projects utilizing over ten thousand nonprofessionals in a wide range of settings throughout the United States.[5]

The research findings are derived mainly from a comprehensive, 17-page mail questionnaire to which 185 project directors provided information concerning their programs and their utilization of nonprofessionals in mental health service roles. Although the survey is basically descriptive, analysis also appears along with informal evaluation based on the project directors' assessments of the advantages and problems of nonprofessional manpower. A selected number of personal site-visit interviews (with project directors) were conducted within the New York metropolitan area to add depth and specificity to the study.

Generally, data on nonprofessionals was organized on the basis of whether the nonprofessional was paid or not, his job-title, and functions performed. Data was individualized so that

---

[5] Project is defined in Chapter 3.

each of the 185 projects could be characterized in terms of its particular goals and the nature and degree of its preventive and innovative efforts, and nonprofessional activities at specified levels of prevention.

During the period of survey-response (August 1967 through December 1967) the majority of the projects (65 percent) were functioning and anticipating continued operation.[6] Seventy-eight percent of all projects surveyed were in operation from two years to over five years at the time that they responded to the survey—a fact which lends validity to the research because it suggests that the programs were operating a sufficient period of time to allow confident responses.[7]

Fortunately, the response to this survey was excellent (96 percent), and considerable collateral information about non-NIMH facilities was secured to enrich survey findings. As a result, it is suggested that the findings reported in this book reflect most of the experimental and innovative mental health programs which utilized nonprofessionals in this country from 1960 to 1967.[8] This wealth of data, interpreted in the light of the author's practice-experience in the mental health field,

---

[6] The remaining 35 percent had terminated project operation at the time of survey-response; outcome data could often be secured more easily for this group, but other data requiring accurate and complete recall was more difficult to secure from terminated projects.

[7] Probably more important for validity than questions of time of operation were the thorough procedures of checking each questionnaire in terms of its relevance to the study universe, reliability of responses to specific items, and the internal logic of each returned questionnaire. Where necessary, questionnaires were returned for completion or clarification of ambiguities.

[8] It is of interest to note here that some ideas for the use of nonprofessionals in non-NIMH community mental health programs funded by private agencies and other governmental agencies (OEO for example)

allows for wider use of the data than the NIMH project universe to which the mail survey was addressed.

Nevertheless, this is only a beginning; in the unexplored realm of nonprofessional manpower for mental health prevention and rehabilitation, many important areas could not be studied in this volume. Wherever possible, these are identified throughout the book—but particularly in the last two chapters.

The over-all evidence of this research supports our hopes and suggestions about how mental health programs should help people. In isolated state mental hospitals, in central city community centers, in schools and social agencies caring for the young and the old, the mentally ill, and those particularly vulnerable to emotional disturbance, nonprofessionals are carrying new responsibilities to the surprise and satisfaction of program-directors throughout this country. The critical and innovative role that nonprofessionals are playing in carrying out the nation-wide mental health program could not be imagined before conducting this search. If this book offers a base for further research of this type, its aims will have been fulfilled. And, if its findings and guidelines are seriously considered by mental health planners of the future, then some of today's innovations, herein reported, may expand into confident, forward-moving programs in a less crisis-ridden tomorrow.

---

developed out of earlier NIMH projects. However, the findings of this book do not purport to represent the use of nonprofessionals in the 1,000 or more community action programs funded by OEO in the 1960s.

2

CONCEPTS AND TRENDS
IN MANPOWER
UTILIZATION

In the past few decades, the United States has become increasingly an industrial, technological, and professionally-oriented society. As the professions have grown larger, they have become more specialized. In 1930, for example, 84 percent of the medical school graduates became general practitioners. In 1967 only 2 percent did.[1] This accelerating trend, to acquire and apply new knowledge from the medical and behavioral sciences through specialized professional activity, has also characterized our mental health programs. Psychoanalytic knowledge has been pursued by many in psychiatry, social work, psychology, and nursing in the search for effective intervention techniques.

In mental health not only nonprofessionals but also would-be professionals and those who have achieved minimal professional educational requirements have been encouraged to secure this specialized, clinical, analytically-oriented training in order to qualify to help people in other than the most routine and

---

[1] *The New York Times,* Feb. 11, 1969, p. 1; March 9, 1969, p. 92.

menial functions. The most recent chemotherapy revolution has added still another dimension to the already specialized mental health programs. Understanding the effects of a wide variety of drugs to alleviate symptoms requires a specialized knowledge that is biochemical in nature.

Why then should it become crucial now to spotlight the role of the least-trained and least-specialized worker on the mental health manpower totem pole—the nonprofessional? Has the trend toward greater professional specialization slackened?

The answer, of course, is that more demand for clinically-oriented psychotherapeutic intervention has been created than can possibly be met. Although there has been considerable confusion about the difference between "demand" and "need" for such specialized services, based on how we define these terms, no one seriously claims that available services have been adequate.[2]

In psychiatry it has been estimated that only one-third to one-half of those needed to maintain psychiatric services have been available.[3]

The figures have been even more alarming for social work and nursing services. Particularly in mental health institutions and public welfare and correctional settings, the gap between the demand for highly trained professional staffs and the supply has steadily widened. The lowest ratios of professional mental health personnel to all employees (one to ten) have been found in public hospitals for the mentally ill. Of necessity, then, large

---

[2] *Medical Tribune and Medical News,* Vol. 9, No. 21, Health Manpower: Factors of Crisis, "Definitions Urgently Sought for 'Need-Demand' Gap," March 11, 1968, p. 1.

[3] Daniel Blain, "The Use of People in Mental Health Activities," *Mental Health Manpower,* Vol. II, A Mental Health Planning Study of California Department of Mental Hygiene, June, 1967, p. 81.

numbers of supporting nonprofessionals have had to be recruited to maintain adequate hospital services for the mentally ill.

Moreover, it has become apparent that even the limited supply of clinically trained professionals is unevenly distributed throughout the country. For example, as late as 1964 there were no psychiatrists and no formal mental health programs in 75 percent of the nation's counties.[4] Studies by Hollingshead and Redlich, and others have focused attention on the inhumane distribution of psychotherapeutically trained professionals along economic levels and social-class lines. Inhabitants of rural areas, urban ghetto dwellers, lower-class working people, and minority groups have been shown to be practically untouched by professional mental health services.

As the distance between articulated need and available professional personnel resources has widened, mental health has remained no longer the exclusive province of the professional specialist. The services of others have been urgently enlisted: clergymen, teachers, and the professionals who were not trained in mental health—people without professional qualifications and with limited educational backgrounds, willing to serve without being paid yet eager to help bring services to those in need of professional expertise. Thus, the scarce professional acquired still another task—supervision of a new manpower source—the most numerous of whom were the nonprofessionals.

Although it may appear that the trend toward greater specialization has slackened, in reality that trend has continued while a new one—the use of nonprofessionals—has forced us to take notice.

---

[4] It should be noted, however, that some of these counties are very sparsely populated.

It would be misleading to suggest that this change has been initiated entirely by the mental health profession. Many other social and cultural changes have occurred which have had important effects on the concept of mental health programs. To better understand these changes, and, particularly, how they have brought forth innovations in manpower utilization, we need to look at a number of broad, related social trends. Then we want to examine changing priorities and concepts of care within the mental health field. Finally, we want to consider how the employment of a larger number of new roles is challenging the traditional ideas of how labor and authority between professionals and nonprofessionals should be divided, and how the effectiveness of the entire system of mental health services is thereby influenced.

SOCIAL TRENDS

Although it is not within the scope of this book to attempt a thorough analysis of all the streams of influence which have converged to create mental health manpower shortages, and the utilization of nonprofessionals, the consensus is that the following factors are the determining ones.

OVER-ALL MANPOWER NEEDS

The shortage of available mental health manpower is linked to this country's over-all manpower problem, which is exceedingly complex and interwoven with the nation's economic and social fabric. In the coming years this problem, no doubt, will attract considerable attention in government planning. No professional discipline in America today is producing enough graduates to keep up with population increases. While the birth rate has been constantly rising, the death rate has declined, creating a changing age distribution in our society. The increase in the number of young people who reach age 18 each year is especially dramatic, and the relative percentage of those over 65 is greater than at any time in the past.

Couple this picture of an expanding population with the movement from rural to urban areas (thanks to automated agricultural production), and the changing emphasis in the nation's labor force from blue- to white-collar and from relatively unskilled to highly skilled, and we see all too clearly a compound problem of unemployable, unskilled, young, minority, ex-rural, and aged, clustering in cities. To further complicate manpower problems, shortages are particularly acute in those fields which are growing most rapidly—education and health services. These services require the highest levels of education and training, but average annual salaries tend to be low for nurses, social workers, and teachers, barely matching services such as law enforcement and transportation (which require considerably less investment in education and training). Thus, we see the teaching and health professions, including, of course, mental health professions, competing in the same limited pool of educational recruits with many disadvantages.

Fortunately, most planners have begun to see more clearly the connection between expanded health and education services and the overall health of the nation's economy, which requires that the necessary manpower for growth not only be available but also that it be employed.

This goal is embodied in the Health Professions Educational Assistance Act of 1963. This act, as well as subsequent health manpower legislation, has provided critical financial assistance to expand training facilities for the health professions over the next decade. Social workers, public health, and other professional workers are expected to play a constructive role in implementing the national economic goal of an active manpower policy to eliminate youth unemployment, minority group unemployment, underemployment, poverty, and other economic ills. It is hoped that from this and similar programs, needed research and experimentation will help alleviate the nation's overall manpower needs.

Another factor contributing to manpower problems is the disintegration of the traditional stabilizing family unit. The aged are often left to fare for themselves, the unskilled minorities are without economic muscle, and the young are without a ready entry into the labor force. Two major social trends, poverty and social isolation, which have become apparent in the last decade, indicate clearly why public and mental health services are in the vanguard of forces attempting to solve the national manpower problems.

CHANGE IN CONCEPT OF POVERTY

There is a growing awareness of "The Other America"—the poor existing amidst an economy of plenty, but failing to receive the benefits of socioeconomic, medical, and psychological knowledge and services already accessible to the growing middle class. The Johnson Administration's "War on Poverty" highlighted proposals to redistribute programs and services, and to utilize in this endeavor the poor, untrained, and "indigenous" themselves in the role of professional. This campaign—influenced by the Civil Rights movement, growing cleavage between blacks and whites, and concepts of black power—exposed the beleaguered "Other America"—a predominantly black America which desperately needs improved job opportunities, education, housing, and overall mental health and social services.

21

In addressing the redistribution of social and mental health services to disadvantaged groups, different models of care and divisions of roles began to appear. Models of institutional change, social competence, social learning, and political power have been offered in rapid succession as more compatible to the needs of these groups than traditional medical and social care models.

Although these models have not been sufficiently tested to establish their superiority over older models of care, there is considerable agreement that the utilization of the poor, the untrained, the neighborhood nonprofessional has already proved of value in reducing social distance between the middle class professional and the poor person with a vastly different life style. Many are convinced that better contact can be made initially with someone who shares one's background, and that important bridging and expediting roles can be performed by these groups. No scientific evidence has appeared, however, to indicate that the ability to sustain communication with another person and to offer wise counsel is necessarily enhanced by shared class background.

The problems of the poor are beginning to be recognized as extraordinarily complex. A link between poverty and mental illness is suggested by recent findings from a study of relief rolls in Santa Barbara, California. A survey, undertaken to verify social workers' impressions that they were dealing with increasing numbers of mentally ill persons, showed that more than one of every four welfare recipients in the county had a diagnosed psychiatric disability, and one in seven had spent time in a mental hospital.[5] This report concluded that the pressures of coping with so many persons both poor and emotionally dis-

[5] Harry Nelson, "The High Ratio of Mentally Ill Found in California Relief Study," *The New York Post*, May 29, 1968, p. 14.

turbed made the social worker's job one of the most demanding in county government. It also predicted that an increase in both the number and the severity of psychiatric problems handled by welfare social workers would parallel the trend toward keeping psychiatric cases in the community instead of confining them to state hospitals.

Expectations that nonprofessionals, indigenous or not, could take full responsibility for handling some of these thorny problems began to appear unrealistic. Still, there have been promising reports of important contributions being made by nonprofessionals working with the poor.

Under such titles as neighborhood agent, enabler, reach-out aide, advocate, expediter, and liaison aide, a variety of activities have been recognized as meaningful. Among such activities are informal socializing, informational, resource-finding, and lay interpretive.

Use of the poor to rehabilitate the poor has reinforced the value pattern of nonprofessional utilization, the self-help model of extending aid to another person who shares one's particular problem—the ex-alcoholic, the ex-addict, the ex-offender, the former mental patient. In the process it was hoped that the ex-patient would aid in his own rehabilitation (the "helper therapy" principle) and be trained for jobs not subject to automation.[6] Although it is reported that considerable numbers of ex-offenders are being trained as group counseling leaders in correctional institutions following "social work" models, little evidence exists that such help is effective for either the offender or the ex-offender. However, what has been discovered is that two variables appear related to the success of the offender

---

[6] Frank Riessman, "The Helper Therapy Principle," *Social Work*, Vol. 10, No. 2, April 1965.

trainee in counseling: (1) that the trainee likes people, and has an ability to work with them and gain their respect; and (2) any program must be accompanied by intensive in-service training and counseling programs.[7]

SOCIAL ISOLATION IN MODERN TIMES

Unlike poverty, which by definition haunts a particular class, the growing impersonality and isolation in this age of the nuclear family affects all economic levels and classes. For rich and poor alike, the primary family group offers less emotional support at critical periods of life than it once did. Although we have little reliable data with which to make comparisons, there is general agreement that the phenomenon of social isolation has become an endemic problem in the community. The cruelty of enforced retirement of some individuals in their early sixties has yet to be faced.

Our increasingly automated society is generating more leisure time for young and old alike; the "Year 2000" is expected to bring still more free time for young and old alike, leisure which will condemn many to pastures of empty boredom unless productive avenues of citizen participation are created.

Yet, this same group of people includes vast numbers of individuals of all ages who are capable of reaching out to befriend and help other human beings in need of friendship and emotional support. Thus, we see a return in modern dress of the earliest untrained social worker of the nineteenth century called the "friendly visitor" (and described so well by Mary Richmond), now attired with similar titles: home visitor, com-

---

[7] Pros and Cons: New Roles for Nonprofessionals in Corrections, U.S. Department of Health, Education and Welfare, U.S. Government Printing Office, Washington, D.C., 1966, pp. 103-4.

panion, big brother, community mental health aide, foster parent, neighborhood aide. These titles tell the tale of the nonprofessional citizen's role in combating involuntary alienation in the community.

As the National Assembly on Mental Health Education proclaimed some years ago,

any volunteer activity—visiting hospitals, helping in rehabilitation—will lead to greater support for and greater advances in positive mental health than intellectually oriented mental health educational programs. Not only do people learn by feeling and doing, but their sympathies tend to be holistic. They may become identified with the mental health movement through volunteer activities, learn to define it as "good" and heartily support all its activities, starting with the mentally ill and encompassing efforts in "positive" mental health education.[8]

There is evidence, too, of the contribution volunteers can make in attacking social problems in concert with community neighbors, and of the unique value of service, given without monetary reward, in terms of its impact on the volunteer and the ones he serves. Volunteer status, however, does present special problems, particularly in large bureaucratic organizations. Utilization of volunteers who are completely free to determine the amount of time they will give to their work activities can have an effect on efficiency standards in mental health service delivery.

Nevertheless, a recent study of the use of volunteers in public welfare concluded that the advantages inherent in involving citizens as volunteers in public welfare programs outweighed the disadvantages. Patients in one mental hospital who

---

[8] *Mental Health Education: A Critique,* Pennsylvania Mental Health, Inc. (Phila., 1960), p. 38.

evaluated the value of all activities on their behalf rated volunteer companionship as more favorable than all other activities in 22 out of 29 instances. This type of evidence supports the increasingly acknowledged belief that social isolation is a crucial factor not only in the etiology of mental illness but also in its perpetuation.

Out of earlier study of sensory deprivation (particularly the effect of separation of mother and child) has evolved the belief that social deprivation is highly detrimental to mental health, and that treatment and rehabilitation programs must work toward reversing patterns of isolation.

We have described briefly the broad link between economic poverty, the social poverty of isolation in modern life, and the kinds of roles nonprofessionals can play in the solutions to these social problems. Now we want to consider some of the issues involved in utilizing nonprofessionals within the changing framework of concepts underlying the treatment and prevention of mental illness in the relatively young field of community psychiatry.

NONPROFESSIONALS IN TREATMENT AND REHABILITATION
OF THE MENTALLY ILL
(TERTIARY LEVEL OF PREVENTION)

The term "tertiary prevention" may appear euphemistic when applied to those who have already succumbed to serious mental illnesses. A valid rationale for its use appears, however, when one considers that effective treatment of the most seriously ill can limit their disabilities and prevent chronic impairment. Manpower needs in the treatment and rehabilitation of acute and chronic mental illness are highly visible. Any family faced

26

with such illness in one of its members can attest to a critical need for outside intervention.

Mental illness, which affects about one in every ten persons to some degree at some time of life, is considered by many to be one of the nation's largest health problems.[9] Although the advent of drug therapy has gradually decreased the number of patients in mental hospitals over the last few years, part of this decrease is attributed to the fact that patients who, ten years ago, would have been banished quietly to state institutions are now being treated in community clinics, the psychiatric units of general hospitals, and private mental hospitals. As a result, a growing proportion of the population of state mental hospitals are the hard-core schizophrenic patients, requiring extensive care and rehabilitation services.

Currently, about 20 percent of first admissions to state and county mental hospitals, are patients with schizophrenia.[10] Their relative youth at admission and the relatively low death rate of these patients are factors which combine to increase the percentage of such patients up to more than half the resident population of state and county mental hospitals. For such ego-damaged patients chemotherapy and psychotherapy are not sufficient to prevent further deterioration.

Milieu therapy programs have been devised in recent years to provide a productive, structured environment in which hos-

---

[9] A recent survey of public attitudes toward the mentally ill revealed that New York City adults rated mental illness as the nation's greatest health problem. (*Public Image of Mental Health Service,* Elinson, Padilla, and Perkins, N.Y.C. Community Mental Health Board, Mental Health Materials Center, N.Y., 1967.)

[10] Howard A. Rusk, "New Mental Center," *The New York Times,* April 21, 1968, p. 58. Also, Mental Health Statistics of U.S. Department of Health, Education and Welfare, 1966-1967.

pital patients can learn and experiment with social and vocational attitudes and skills necessary for resumption of life in the community. A wide spectrum of services is projected, based on these newer concepts of the therapeutic milieu: group and individual counseling, self-government by patients, retraining in everyday activities such as personal hygiene, dining, and shopping, and conversation. An essential component of the new rehabilitation clubs and centers are therapy programs designed to prepare patients for vocational training which can help them adjust to community life after discharge.

Paid and volunteer nonprofessionals have long been used in mental hospitals. However, the depressing atmosphere of most state hospitals has not been conducive to the recruitment of either group. Negative attitudes toward mental illness and the low status and wage scales of nonprofessional personnel has frustrated large-scale programs to utilize ward attendants, nurses, and other nonprofessional aides.

Today, however, the nonprofessional aide is recognized as the first line of contact with the patient. The aide in the therapeutic milieu is considered as a therapeutic agent, guide, companion, and above all an essential facilitator in the patient's daily treatment and rehabilitation. In many hospitals, it is reported that the aide communicates with the patients far better than do the doctors.[11] With in-service training programs and utilization of new types of persons (for example, college students), it has become possible to plan for extensive manpower utilization programs to provide more therapeutic milieu and rehabilitation programs for the mentally ill.

As we have clearly indicated, there is no lack of appreciation for the goals of therapeutic intervention for those who are

---

[11] Elaine and John Cummings, *Ego and Milieu*, Atherton Press, New York, 1962, p. 156.

mentally ill. But the study and application of measures to intervene before a problem is manifest (primary prevention), or in the earliest stages of disorder (secondary prevention), have lagged far behind therapeutic measures. Manpower shortages should not be permitted to delay further a preventive program aiming for total "well" communities and target populations within them. Approaching the source of the mental health problem is more likely to decrease it than all projected manpower solutions.

NONPROFESSIONALS IN PROMOTION OF COMMUNITY MENTAL HEALTH (PRIMARY PREVENTION)

The concept of primary prevention emphasizes promotion of the general health of the community and reduction of the incidence of mental illness not for individuals one-by-one, but rather by increasing the total proportion of well to sick in the population. Despite exhortations by leaders and their periodically valiant, innovative efforts, remarkably little has been done systematically at this highest level of prevention.

Funding for prevention has been almost nil, partly because of the acute day-by-day service needs of the mentally ill. Planning has heretofore concentrated on service either for those already designated as mentally ill through mental hospitals or for those designated as needy through public welfare agencies, with the focus on relief-giving, provision of foster homes, institutions, and protective service arrangements for the most deviant or the few most needy and ill in the community.

The token development in most areas of this country of basic preventive resources and services considered important in promoting and maintaining family mental health (for example, comprehensive prenatal and postnatal care programs, parent education for child rearing, homemaking, and day care) testifies to the limited involvement of both professional and nonprofessional personnel in the well-being and mental health of families and children.

Several factors handicap primary prevention efforts. First, the effects of promoting and protecting mental health are not highly visible to the community. It demands a higher level of imagination and foresight to plan prevention of a disorder than to pick up the pieces as they fall. Second, even among professionals there has been little agreement on what to prevent and how to prevent it. Some conceive of primary prevention chiefly in terms of changing institutions; others see individual citizens (not institutions) as needing change; and still others believe that an integrated model of clinical and social systems skills is needed to truly promote mental health.[12]

Eliminate poverty, the first group maintains, and you will witness a reduction in the proportion of the mentally ill population. Substitute income maintenance programs for our obsolete welfare system and you will do more to improve the nation's mental health than all the country's case-by-case therapeutic and social service programs combined.

But man does not live by bread alone, the second group contends. The need to be loved, and to develop one's unique potential from infancy on through old age, is a compelling one, requiring that the family improve its ability to provide a stable,

---

[12] Gerald Caplan, *An Approach to Community Mental Health,* Grune and Stratton, New York, 1961: Robert Reiff, "Mental Health Manpower and Institutional Change," paper presented at the University of Rochester Conference on Emergent Approaches to Mental Health Programs (June 17-19, 1965); and Alfred J. Kahn, *Exploratory Essays in Social Welfare Planning,* Columbia University School of Social Work Library, Mimeo., 1962.

loving atmosphere in which mentally healthy members can grow. Guidance and counseling to individuals and families, anticipating problems at crucial times of one's life (school entry, adolescence, marriage, pregnancy, retirement, etc.) and during accidental crises (for example, illness, unemployment) offer the most effective means to promote and maintain family mental health.

Individuals and institutions need to change in unison, still others explain. Programs must be comprehensive enough to improve provision of basic emotional supplies for all people with concrete built-in opportunities which encourage them to articulate needed changes and to work toward such changes in the major institutions which shape their lives.

Despite emphasis on the need for primary prevention, outlined in the Mental Health Study Act of 1955 and reinforced by subsequent presidential messages, this level of prevention remains unformulated. As indicated in Chapter 1, the Joint Commission on Mental Illness and Health decided as recently as 1961 to focus on the needs of the acutely mentally ill and to leave mental health promotion and "primary prevention" programs for a day when greater knowledge or something akin to the pharmaceutical revolution would ensure practical success in such programs.[13]

But communities may not be willing to wait. The Community Mental Health Centers Act of 1963 was concerned with "high risk" populations and the "well" population—the 90 percent in need of practical mental health information and assistance. Ecological and crisis theories formulated by mental health investigators such as Eric Lindemann, Eric Erikson, Gerald Caplan, and others identified with the community men-

---

[13] *Action for Mental Health,* Basic Books, New York, 1961, pp. 242-43.

tal health movement, provide a framework for helping people to cope with expected life crises (birth, school entry) and accidental life crises (an infant's loss of its mother, a wage earner's loss of job).

The knowledge of the dynamic interplay between the individual and his environment suggests action on behalf of individuals and whole populations in stress situations. Specific knowledge of the phenomenon of crisis, its phases and timing, teaches that a little help at the right time is more preventive than long-term help initiated toward the end of a crisis period.[14] Vital biological, social, and cultural "supplies" are viewed as essential in certain critical periods of life.

Certain supplies need to be given very early in life; others are more crucial during adolescence, adulthood, or old age. (René Dubos reports experiences in Guatemala which demonstrated that when children from Indian Villages are taken at the age of four to an experimental school and fed a good diet, it is *too late* to correct biological deficiencies which have already developed.)[15] The long-term view of human development and the short-term view of crisis provide a macroscopic model for planning preventive services.[16]

The possibilities for nonprofessional utilization in primary prevention have hardly been contemplated. The nation is just beginning to deal with one of its most serious and persistent preventive mental health problems, the "deprivation syndrome"

---

[14] Lydia Rapoport, "Working with Families in Crisis: An Exploration in Preventive Intervention," *Social Work*, Vol. 7, 3:48-56, July 1962.

[15] "Dubos wins American Nobel Prize," *The New York Times*, Oct. 5, 1966. Based on report of the Pan American Health Organization, Advisory Council on Medical Research, p. 1.

[16] Gerald Caplan, *An Approach to Community Mental Health*, pp. 31-34.

in infants and children to whom the biopsychosocial necessities for normal growth and development are unavailable.[17] The negative teenager, the lonely, lost older person, are also candidates for new programs using nonprofessional personnel. As the Community Mental Health Center Movement claims responsibility for all social groups, all age groups, the sick and the well, nonprofessionals will be enlisted in preventive roles. The paid or volunteer teacher mom who provides a needed relationship for a socially deprived child, the counselor in a store-front mental health agency who helps poor families with the daily stresses of living, the foster grandparent who cares regularly for the neglected, hospitalized child, the community organizer who enlists aged citizens in community improvement programs, the homemaker who keeps the family and home intact when a mother becomes ill—these are practical demonstrations which suggest ways of decreasing the need for professional therapeutic intervention if nonprofessionals extend a helping hand without waiting for mental illness to strike.

NONPROFESSIONALS IN EARLY DETECTION
OF MENTAL DISORDER (SECONDARY PREVENTION)

Closely allied, but with an independent emphasis, are programs of early case findings and diagnoses which characterize the level of secondary prevention.[18]

---

[17] President Johnson's Message to Congress asking additional funds to prevent early childhood neglect. This suggested new uses of neighborhood child care experts and indigenous child health aides in disadvantaged areas. *The New York Times*, Feb. 9, 1968, p. 1.

[18] See Chapter 7 for further discussion of relationships between levels. Full discussion of this issue can be found in Caplan, *Principles of Preventive Psychiatry*, pp. 89-113.

Secondary prevention implies early detection, both in the life cycle of the individual and in the course of the particular disorder. Epidemiological studies and large-scale screening programs form the base for such operations. Such institutions as schools have vast and hardly explored potential for early detection and secondary prevention of emotional disorder. The community mental health center is expected, too, to become increasingly concerned with earlier case finding and referral. Emergency services are considered indispensable in offering first aid for all types of budding disorder.

The possibility exists of training nonprofessionals to detect signs of pathology, to refer clients to appropriate facilities, and to offer other interventions when facilities are not available. A serious problem may be presented if the treatment facilities of a community are limited, and more cases are uncovered than can be adequately treated.

One solution to this problem has been to train mental health aides to develop treatment skills. It must be asked, however, whether the treatment role is truly appropriate for a nonprofessional. A little treatment by ill-equipped staff can be worse than no treatment at all. Obviously, training and supervisory programs would need to be part of secondary prevention if nonprofessionals begin to take on substantial treatment roles in neighborhood and community mental health centers.

PROGRAM PLANNING, STATUS, AND POWER ISSUES

Some broad social trends and specific trends in mental health care have been considered in relation to new manpower uses. Many other issues remain, and some of them will be raised here.

Looking strictly at objectives in the use of nonprofessionals in mental health, one finds a questionable mixture of conflicting goals, often lacking in priorities. Unable to wait for research-based knowledge, some large-scale programs have emerged, combining ambitious and often contradictory goals. A major dilemma has been to clarify which deserves highest priority: the needs of patients and community citizens served by the programs, or the needs of disadvantaged citizens to escape poverty through employment in human service occupations. In the latter, one's eye focuses first on creating jobs within the organizational structure which will offer personal and occupational opportunity for the poor and other deprived groups to advance in society. Recruitment, training, and job roles are necessarily influenced. If employment is the primary goal, the professional reacts with understandable guilt when he must fire an incompetent nonprofessional. Carried to the extreme, one is moving toward the creation of a welfare system, although a new and possibly more constructive job welfare system.

Yet, if improved service to patients and to community is the key goal, a different set of considerations prevails in the use of nonprofessionals. One's concern is whether nonprofessionals can help to alleviate acute staff shortages, energize the existing professions, and provide new or "unique" services, thereby improving the quality of service to individuals and communities. Again, we are faced with a mixed blend of objectives. Few professionals can agree on priorities in planning improved services. Even if they could, funding sources shape the course of mental health programs and manpower use to a much greater degree than professional opinion. **1536251**

Assuming that our primary objective should be to enrich mental health programs, and that we agree on how to do this, a hard look must still be taken at the obstacles of professional-nonprofessional interaction which appear as one commits oneself to the use of nonprofessionals. If the nonprofessional feels that his performance equals that of the professional, he gains the confidence to ask for equal pay. (This occurred in New York City in a Mobilization for Youth project when nonprofessional community organizers saw little difference between their performance and that of professionals.) Similarly, at Lincoln Hospital's Mental Health Service Program in the Bronx, New York, some professionals were chagrined to find that the nonprofessionals argued successfully that only they should serve as delegates to a poverty convention, disclaiming the need for professional opinions to represent the agency.[19] By the spring of 1969, the nonprofessional staff had developed the power to precipitate a crisis which culminated in a change in the professional leadership of the hospital program.

The professions have spent years in carefully developing strict educational standards and fighting nonspecific qualifications which lead to personal and political favoritism. For many (such as the professional social workers of the Veterans Administration) it has been an uphill fight to achieve recognition of professional status and to keep up with the higher status of physicians, psychologists, and other professional teammates. Competition from nonprofessional social workers, arriving at a time of newly achieved professional status for social workers within the system, is not likely to be welcomed.

Conflict is sharpest as the nonprofessional moves closer in training and job responsibility to his professional colleague. That is, the professional feels threatened by the prospect of a

---

[19] "Issues and Strategies in the Use of Nonprofessionals." Speech presented by Emanuel Hallowitz, Director of Neighborhood Service Center Program of Lincoln Hospital Mental Health Service at National Association of Social Workers Symposium, National Conference of Social Welfare, San Francisco, May 25, 1968.

career line which may rival his own, as between the professionally trained (master of social work degree) social worker and the college graduate social worker, especially when both are assigned similar job responsibility. In medical circles a storm of protest arose following a proposal for the development of a physician's assistant (master's degree educational level) who could be expected to earn a salary close to that of the average physician. There was less evidence of opposition to career lines of physicians' assistants at lower levels—those with high school diploma or community college background.

Obviously, the absolute power of the professional establishment has been breached. As the nonprofessional is called in to help the professional who is under attack for failing to provide adequate service to the mentally ill and to the poor, he reacts first with pleasure and hope for prestige in his association with the professional. But, even before his disappointment at not getting a quick and equal share of the pie begins to set in, some disturbing questions need to be posed.

For example, in Neighborhood Service Centers and state hospitals, is the nonprofessional to become the poor man's therapist? That is, are we offering inferior, untrained social workers and psychiatrists to the poor? And, if this is true, is this an expedient which is morally acceptable to mental health planners and to the community?

Are we rationalizing our exploitation of those gifted nonprofessionals whose performances rise rapidly with training on the grounds that they are serving only the previously unserved poor, and that, anyhow, they lack proper educational credentials?

One answer to the charge of exploitation of the "new nonprofessional" is to be found in the "New Careers" movement, a coalition of nonprofessionals supported by professionals and administrators dedicated to upgrading the nonprofessionals' status through training tied to career lines.[20] Nonprofessionals in career-entry jobs are beginning to seek labor union support.[21] In June 1968 a dramatic answer to the charge of exploitation was heard at Topeka State Hospital in Kansas. In an unusual strike, sixty psychiatric aides and other "serfs of the Kansas mental hospital system"[22] seized administrative control of eight wards and proceeded to demonstrate how a hospital ward should be run. Patients were given needed individual attention by extra aides placed in each ward, and signs were posted saying: "This is a Union-Administered Ward." The point was made that proper patient care depended on giving nonprofessionals a larger and well-deserved share of economic power.

Implicit in the fight for greater power within the establishment is the suggestion that professional power should be diminished. Instead of raising money to get better professionals, would it not be less expensive and more efficient to train and upgrade more aides in mental health work?[23] (Indeed, despite turnover, it is usually easy to recruit psychiatric aides.) Having entered the human services occupations, the nonprofessional is not always impressed by the "emperor's new clothes." He questions methods, techniques, and professional commitment to individual patient and to community improvement. The lack of sharp demarcation between professional and nonprofessional roles in mental health and allied disciplines (notably, social

---

[20] Frank Riessman, "The New Careers Concept," in *American Child*, No. 1, Winter 1967, pp. 2-8.

[21] New Careers Newsletter.

[22] Alex Efthim, "The Nonprofessionals Revolt," *The Nation*, August 5, 1968.

[23] *Ibid.*

work, nursing, and teaching) is emphasized in some quarters seeking power for nonprofessionals.

This fire is readily fueled by the assumption of some non-professional leaders that they (rather than the professionals) represent the community—an assumption which became plausible because of the nebulous concept of "community." Without a clear definition of *who* the community is and *how* it governs its constituents, this power struggle can only intensify.

But power will be short-lived if the introduction of the "new nonprofessional" fails in the long run to improve the overall quality of mental health services. Study of more effective use of nonprofessionals working with professionals is urgently required to raise standards of care.

CHANGING MANPOWER ALLOCATION TO IMPROVE QUALITY OF SERVICE

Within the professions, individual researchers and practitioners are attempting to promote a constructive resolution of some of the conflicting interests by addressing the issues of differential utilization of nonprofessionals and professionals.[24]

---

[24] See Bibliography for complete listing. In social work early formulations were presented by Samuel Finestone in "Differential Utilization of Casework Staff in Public Welfare: Major Dimensions," mimeo. paper, May 1964, and by Margaret Heyman in "Effective Utilization of Social Workers in a Hospital Setting," *Hospital, Journal of the American Hospital Association,* Vol. 36, No. 10, May 16, 1965, pp. 44-45. In nursing, the issue has been discussed by Eugene Levine in "Nursing Staffing in Hospitals," the *American Journal of Nursing,* Vol. 61, No. 9, Sept. 1961, and in many, subsequent articles.

Some investigators, notably Barker and Briggs, report that professional social workers (Master of Social Work degree graduates) are not being used optimally or differentially, compared to nonprofessionally trained (college graduate) colleagues.[25]

The B.A. social worker in the state mental hospital is given the same responsibility for caseloads as the M.S.W., but he operates under the handicap of less training and consultation plus the indignity of occupying a lower rung of the hierarchical hospital ladder. Intensive study of the New York City Department of Social Services has led to recent recommendations to reduce the nonprofessionally trained (B.A.) social work staff and to increase the less-educated case-aide staff, those with high school or elementary school background. The latter, many of whom were once welfare recipients themselves, would assist a staff which, it is hoped, would contain a higher proportion of the fully professional (master's degree) social workers.

Automation has cut the need for the massive paperwork and the holding operations which formerly characterized the job of the B.A. welfare worker. The greater diagnostic and planning skills of the M.S.W. social worker, combined with the more concrete, practical action abilities of the lower-level case-aide, are expected to be more effective in tackling the complex range of problems faced by New York City welfare families. In some projects, for example, a Neighborhood Service Project in Washington, D.C., it has been found that social work skills are not necessary to reach out and direct poor families to community health resources.

Moreover, neighborly health aides can learn to cut red tape

[25] Robert L. Barker, and Thomas Briggs, "Differential Utilization of Social Work Personnel," National Association of Social Workers, New York, 1968.

as efficiently as professionals, simultaneously becoming more "professional" in their perceptions of themselves as helpers.[26] Similarly, the preliminary reports of a study at one university have shown that approximately 40 percent of the tasks performed by clinical psychologists with doctoral degrees can be competently done by persons with bachelor's degrees and little additional training, if they work under supervision.[27]

Criteria for case and task assignments are being studied and developed.[28] Some practitioners are questioning the viability of the old industrial model (that is, breaking the task down into simplified, standardized tasks) for the helping professions. The point is being made that many professions are moving away from the use of aides for delimited ancillary functions (for example, in nursing, occupational, and physical therapy) since they accumulate successful experience in allowing aides to conduct patients through all steps in rehabilitation.

A project in Wyoming tested the value of rehabilitation counselor aides in assisting with the whole process of vocational rehabilitation. It was not feasible for the agency, which served clients over approximately 30,000 square miles, to divide its job into separate tasks; besides, it was noted that the rehabilitation process is not marked by segmentation. The investigator therefore makes a plea for allowing these counselors to innovate and experiment with the whole rehabilitation process after a short

---

[26] Barbara Heller and Laure Sharp, "Evaluation of the Neighborhood Health Aide Project (1963-1966), Bureau of Social Science Research, Inc., 1200 17th St. N.W., Washington, D.C., November 1966.

[27] Howard A. Rusk, "The Health Message," *The New York Times*, March 10, 1968.

[28] Finestone, Heyman, Barker and Briggs, Levine, et al. See footnotes 24 and 25.

training course, including intensive practical experience.[29]

Agencies with a history of higher percentages of professional social work staff define the nonprofessional's job as completely different from the professional's, while agencies with low percentages of professional social workers (for example, state mental hospitals and child welfare agencies) employ nonprofessionals to carry caseloads with the same responsibility as professionals.[30]

For all investigators, the problem of finding the "simple" case for the untrained remains. The most viable model seems to be the expanded team model. Caseloads can be assigned to teams instead of individuals. Within the teams, professionals and nonprofessionals work together. Some team members might perform strictly administrative jobs; others have partial or total responsibilities.

Preliminary results from experimentation at Connecticut's Valley State Hospital in the organization of different types of teams indicate that the quality and quantity of hospital work output can be increased by changing patterns of use of nonprofessionals and professionals. Rather than the single "case" or task as the unit of responsibility, a cluster of activities based on specified objectives is outlined for the entire team. The team leader, a professional, defines these activities to his nonprofessional associates, encouraging the development of expertise in specific aspects of the activities. The focus of one team was to develop a therapeutic community in the children's unit; various

---

[29] James Calloway, and Robert Kelso, "Don't Handcuff the Aide," *Rehabilitation Record*, March-April 1966, Vol. No. 2, pp. 1-3.

[30] Betty Lacy Jones, "Nonprofessional Workers in Professional Foster Family Agencies," Doctoral Dissertation University of Pennsylvania School of Social Work, University Microfilms, Inc., Ann Arbor Michigan, 1966, p. 116.

recreation and personalized activities were planned to develop in each child a capacity for healthier interpersonal relationships. In other teams, social work "associates" became especially adept in locating farms and homes where patients could live and work under supervision; nursing personnel became experts in developing nursing home placements.[31]

Whatever the setting, the day of the exclusive mental health interdisciplinary team (psychiatrist, psychiatric social worker, psychologist, and nurse in the hospital setting) is drawing to a close. The team has expanded to include other disciplines and allied nonprofessionals who will work to distribute a much wider spectrum of services to many new community groups.

Who does *what* part of the mental health job is a question receiving serious scrutiny. Inevitably, as the balance of power shifts, and depending on the success of nonprofessional efforts to unionize and to gain truly new careers, the able, trained nonprofessional will occupy a seat of considerable importance on the mental health team.

Hopefully, the community (once it is agreed on just *who* constitutes the community and *to what extent* it governs all of us) will then be better able to balance mental health priorities so that professionals and nonprofessionals can work together to provide a network of services to rehabilitate the mentally ill and to safeguard the community's mental health.

---

[31] Barker and Briggs, "Differential Utilization of Social Work Personnel," pp. 246-63.

3

THE NATURE OF
MENTAL HEALTH PROGRAMS

To begin to understand and evaluate the contribution of the nonprofessional to mental health, one must know the work milieu. The 1968 NIMH Project Study provides a comprehensive picture of the work milieu of 185 NIMH-funded projects throughout the country. These accounted for 96 percent of all NIMH-funded projects in which nonprofessionals were engaged in mental health functions. To be sure, there are other mental health programs using nonprofessionals which were not funded by NIMH. However, we have reason to believe that the essential nature of the work environment in other projects was sufficiently similar to that of the NIMH-funded projects to suggest that very many of the findings herein reported (for example, in relation to types of setting, nature of services, and populations served) are relevant to the larger universe of the nation's mental health programs using nonprofessional manpower.

The NIMH Project Study thus gives us a reasonably complete view of the over-all nonprofessional work environment. Since the nature of the work environment greatly determines the functions of the nonprofessionals, it is important that we have a clear view of that environment before we go on to explore nonprofessional functions.

In this chapter we describe the range of mental health projects across the country. What kind of projects are they? Under what auspices are they operated? Where are they located? Whom do they serve? What is the nature of the services given? And what is the proportion of nonprofessionals to professionals in the projects in which they work? These are some of the questions to be answered.

More important, perhaps, is the over-all view of how our efforts are divided among the three levels of primary, secondary, and tertiary preventive goals (an interest discussed in Chapters 1 and 2). What the objectives are in the aggregate view of projects gives us vital clues about the work environment. The reader is referred to Chapter 8 for an in-depth study of project goals which led to the development of a preventive index. It is hoped that this will serve as a guide for mental health planners in correcting imbalances between preventive and treatment efforts.

This over-all perspective not only helps us to better understand the nonprofessionals' work environment, but it also tells us something about how the mental health crisis is being challenged. To what extent are the poor, the minorities, the young and the old in urban and rural settings being helped with the special problems of mental illness, alcoholism, drug addition, or the everyday problems of living? In the aggregate view, we can see more clearly the direction of our energies—the stronger and the weaker spots in the total picture of helping services.

GENERAL PROJECT CHARACTERISTICS

TYPES OF PROJECTS

A mental health project is defined as one in which the paid or volunteer nonprofessional works in a program incorporated in a state mental hospital or into one of the many community settings typically supported by the Mental Health Projects Grant Program of NIMH. All projects in the NIMH Study are (or were) funded by a grant from either the Mental Health Projects Grant Program (MH) or the Hospital Improvement Grant Program (HIP). The Hospital Improvement Grant Program, which in 1964 began new programs on a pilot basis, is designed to improve and upgrade public mental hospitals. Although all HIP projects were planned in relation to the needs of state mental hospitals, a handful of the HIP projects surveyed were located outside the mental hospitals in the interests of providing new services to assist the hospitalized. For example, several were

Table 3.1. Agency Setting According to Grant Program Auspices

| | Grant Auspices | |
Type of Agency Setting	HIP Grants Program	MH Grants Program
Psychiatric hospital	56	26
Educational facility		13
Social agency[a]		12
Multiple other	7	12
Settlement house[b]		11
Community mental health clinic	2	10
Rehabilitation center		7
Public health facility	2	6
General hospital	1	5
Citizen participation organization		4
Specialized hospital	3	3
Correctional agency		3
Mental retardation clinic	1	
Other		1
Total No. of Projects	72	113

[a] Includes public assistance, multifunction, and children's service agencies. Also includes child guidance clinics formally connected with children's service agencies.

[b] Includes more modern version entitled neighborhood development center.

located in community mental health centers, public health facilities, or specialized hospitals (refer to Table 3.1).

In contrast, the Mental Health Projects Grant Program extends grants to a wide variety of agencies, including settlement houses, educational facilities, family agencies, community mental health clinics and centers, public health facilities, and hospitals (both general and specialized). Nor are the auspices of this latter program limited; grants have been given to voluntary agencies, private agencies, and public agencies at the local as well as the state level.

The focus of the MH Projects Grant Program, since its inception in 1956, has been one of broad experimentation and demonstration in the whole range of mental health services; the HIP Grant Program has specialized in efforts to improve the nation's hospital system.

AUSPICES[1]

Sixty-one percent (113) of the projects surveyed are funded through the Mental Health Projects Grant Program, while 39 percent (72) are HIP projects. Thus, for 113 projects out of 185 one can anticipate a variety of project settings and aims reflecting diversified funding policy of the MH Projects Grant

---

[1] NIMH identified each project as funded by the HIP or the MH Program. Agency type and auspice was identified from pretest materials. This data was secured by study of sample listings and from information given in the questionnaire. To fill in data gaps regarding particular agencies, various documents were used, such as the National Directory of Private Social Agencies, Government Organization Manual, Hospital Directory, World Almanac, and progress reports from individual NIMH projects. For example, when it was not clear whether a hospital was general or specialized, this data was secured from the Directory of Hospitals.

Program. However, a significant number of projects (72) are similar, since most are located in state mental hospitals. The sample reflects both diversity and uniformity. Moreover, one can assume that the MH projects are essentially more experimental in character than the HIP projects, which are carried out in the more traditional and structured environment of mental hospitals.[2]

In addition to these funding patterns, the auspices of the sponsoring agency should be considered (refer to Table 3.2).

Table 3.2. Auspices of Sponsoring Agencies

Auspices	Number of Projects	HIP	MH
Public State Agency	97	72	25
Public Local Agency	32		32
Voluntary Agency	41		41
Private Foundation	2		2
Other Auspices Specified	13		13
Total	185	72	113

As one would expect, because of the large number of state hospitals the majority of the projects (52 percent) were under state public auspices. Second were the voluntary, nonprofit, and private agencies and foundations (23 percent). A close third were the local public agencies (17 percent).

However, 13 projects (7 percent) required multiple auspices. For example, one project in New York State required the combined auspices of a state mental hospital, a private vocational rehabilitation agency, and two state rehabilitation and

---

[2] The auspices (HIP vs. MH) are particularly important when we turn to an over-all assessment in Chapter 8, of projects' use of nonprofessionals, especially in relation to whether the projects were currently in operation or terminated projects.

NIMH has also encouraged development of mental health programs in sparsely populated regions and areas in which little had previously been given to people in the way of treatment and prevention facilities.

HOURS OF PROJECT OPERATION AND STAFF AVAILABILITY

Another variable in this overview of the work-milieu of the nonprofessional is the nature of the work schedule of the NIHM projects. The vast majority of projects operate five days a week from 9 to 5. Although nearly half of all projects are located in hospital settings which necessarily maintain a 24-hour-a-day schedule, many of the project services offered to clients (for example, educational, vocational, and retraining) do not require round-the-clock attendance of project staff.

Professionals and nonprofessionals alike work on a regular s with a small proportion having their staff available "on as well. Forty-two projects were open to the public and ed on a 24-hour-a-day basis. It is interesting to note that of 42 projects, 81 percent report that it is their paid nonprofessionals who are available at all times. Professionals are available mostly "on call."

sizeable number of projects report a flexible pattern of and/or weekend hours tailored to the convenience of and other community groups served. A large proportion aff in these projects are available on call.

WORK PATTERNS OF NONPROFESSIONALS

ated, paid nonprofessional staff generally worked eigh day, five days per week, conforming to the usual wor olunteer staff generally worked one or two days pe

employment agencies. In the interest of rehabilitating the mentally ill, and of awakening the community to the need for such programs, professionals and nonprofessionals teamed up within the hospital to prepare patients for employment after discharge. They also went out into the community, seeking a suitable vocational climate for their patients and stimulating citizen participation in similar projects.

TYPES OF AGENCIES

In identifying agency types, the concern was with the setting of the sponsoring agency; for example, an NIMH project which consisted of an after-school clinic program for emotionally disturbed children, located and sponsored in a settlement house, was classified as a "settlement house" rather than a "mental health" clinic. If service was given in more than one type of agency, the heading of "multiple settings" was used.

As would be expected, the largest single group of projects are located in psychiatric hospitals. Forty-four percent of the projects (82) are in mental hospitals, and 10 percent (19) are located in more than one type of setting. Examples of multiple settings are a correctional agency and a rehabilitation center, and a cooperative venture between community agencies, a university, and a hospital.

Educational facilities are the settings for the second largest group of projects (13). Community mental health clinics and settlement houses (or neighborhood development centers) and social agencies (including family, children's service, multifunction, and public assistance agencies) account for similar numbers of projects (11 and 12). For a complete breakdown, refer to Table 3.1.

It should be noted that this distribution probably does not

accurately reflect the actual composition of settings for mental health programs. For example, we know that hospitals and universities were quick to request funds from NIMH, whereas outpatient clinics and social agencies were slower and more infrequent in their requests.

Although at the present time the Community Mental Health Centers Act is stimulating the use of funds in community mental health clinics and other outpatient settings, this could not possibly be reflected significantly in the study population. Possibly the major reason for the skewed distribution in favor of hospitals is that there is a long history of use of volunteers and paid nonprofessionals in hospitals. The hospital setting, with its past emphasis on custodial care, has always lent itself to recruitment and use of paid nonprofessionals. In addition, there has been traditionally more space and facilities for use of volunteers in hospital buildings than in outpatient service facilities.

Other factors are the high visibility of the hospital as a setting for mental health work by volunteers, and its dramatic quality. Possibly the more obvious, gross need of inpatients for aid of various types has made it easier for volunteers to become motivated to aid in hospital mental health work, and the range of needs of inpatients has always offered a greater variety of possible services that volunteers might contribute—the whole gamut of living experiences within a highly structured environment.

GEOGRAPHIC FACTORS AND REGION
OF PROJECT LOCATION

The locations of the NIMH projects are distributed throughout the regions of the United States. In terms of a regional organization pattern suggested by the United States Census Bureau of

the Budget, there is a fairly even distribution of NIMH One-third of the projects are clustered in the Northea compared with one-fifth of the projects located in th little less than one-half of the projects were evenly (tween the North Central and Southern regions.

POPULATION OF CITY OF PROJECT LO

Populations of towns and cities represented in th' from under 2,500 population to the largest (500,000 population (refer to Table 3.3). One-'

Table 3.3. Number and Percent of NIMF Population of City

Population of City of Project Location	Number of Projects
Over 500,000[a]	61
100,000–499,000	28
25,000–99,999	32
2,500–24,999	31
Under 2,500	33
Total	185

[a] Suburban areas contiguous to and int with the particular urban area.

jects (61) are located in or around ulation of over 500,000. This is ha the United States when one cor of the lower-income urban popu' tan areas, which are confronte breakdown in family structure of social and medical proble health.

week and from one to four hours per day. Reports of unusually long work hours were found in cottage counselor and other "substitute mother" jobs which cannot conform to the usual time schedules.

NONPROFESSIONALS AND PROFESSIONALS COMPARED[3]

Considering all projects together, the over-all ratio is six nonprofessional persons to one professional (6:1). The majority of projects (59 percent) employed more nonprofessionals than professionals. For all projects combined, the over-all ratio is eight work hours of nonprofessional time to one work hour of professional time (8:1). Considering paid nonprofessional hours separately, this ratio is six hours to one professional work hour. Most of the volunteers typically work fewer hours per week than their paid counterparts; the ratio of volunteer hours to professional hours is therefore considerably lower than the of paid nonprofessionals.

RATIO PATTERNS IN SELECTED PROJECT
CHARACTERISTICS

The relationships between selected project characteristics and the ratio of nonprofessionals to professionals revealed some interresting facts. The relationship between size of city (of project location) and the ratio of nonprofessionals indicated that the highest ratios of paid nonprofessionals are not found predomin-

---

[3] Data on number of persons employed and estimates of time worked were secured in the survey. Several ratios were computed. High ratio meant employment of three times as many nonprofessionals as professionals (or more). Low ratio meant that the project employed fewer nonprofessionals than professionals. The same applied to the ratio of hours worked.

antly in the largest metropolitan cities of 500,000 or more population; rather, two-thirds of the projects with high ratios of paid nonprofessionals are almost equally distributed between small towns and cities (populations of 2,500 to under 25,000) and the medium and larger cities (25,000 to under 500,000). For most of the projects the ratios of volunteers to professionals are uniformly low in rural and urban areas, small and large cities.

Between type of agency setting and ratio of nonprofessionals, a highly significant, clear relationship exists for the ratio of nonprofessionals in the various types of settings in which the projects are located. Medium and high ratios of paid nonprofessionals are found predominantly (70 percent) in institutional care settings. The opposite is true for community settings: low ratios (or no paid nonprofessionals at all) predominate in community settings. Ratios of volunteers to professionals tend to be low in all settings.

SERVICES GIVEN BY PROFESSIONAL STAFF

Today, as in the past, the direction of the mental health agencies has been considered the primary responsibility of trained mental health professionals. Although mental health professionals now include teachers, sociologists, and anthropologists, and nonprofessionals are rapidly entering the mental health team, leadership of NIMH projects is still with the major mental health disciplines—psychiatrists, social workers, and psychologists. Social workers constitute the largest single professional discipline while psychologists are a close second.

All of the major mental health disciplines are concerned chiefly with providing direct service to patients and community groups. Three quarters of professional staff time is devoted to direct services. On the average, one-fifth of professional time is spent on combined training and supervision of nonprofessionals to improve the quantity and quality of mental health services.

PRIOR USE OF NONPROFESSIONALS

Most of the projects reported that their sponsoring agency had previously utilized nonprofessionals. The single most popular job title reflecting prior use was Recreation and Group Work Aide (this applies to both paid and volunteer workers). For paid workers alone, nursing and ward personnel had previously worked in more projects than any other paid title. For all the other traditional job titles, most projects tended previously to have hired paid nonprofessionals only. However, for the more innovative titles (for example, community mental health aide), volunteers were used almost exclusively in the past. Volunteer teacher aide was the most widely mentioned innovative title reflecting previous use.

PRIOR USE BY AUSPICE

Eighty-six percent of the HIP projects reported prior use of nonprofessionals as compared to 75 percent of the MH projects. Since the bulk of the HIP projects are located in hospitals which have traditionally utilized nonprofessionals, this difference is to be expected.

PRIOR USE BY SETTING

One could have anticipated that there would be a significant relationship between type of agency and prior use of nonprofessionals. Particularly in projects located in institutional care settings, there was a strong tendency to have used nonprofessionals. The reverse pattern was found in community settings, such as in social agencies.

PROJECT POPULATIONS AND TYPES OF CARE PROVIDED

Knowledge about the populations served by the NIMH projects, and the nature of the care given to them, is highly relevant to understanding the work of nonprofessionals. Project populations include the patients, clients, consultee groups, or entire community entities served collectively or individually in the NIMH projects. Types of care encompass the whole range of care-systems serving the project populations in hospitals, clinics, social agencies, schools, and other community settings. Such types of care range from traditional hospital care to the newer types of community out-reach care—namely, day hospital, half-way house, home care, and store front center care.

DIMENSIONS OF POPULATION AND TYPES OF CARE

A major distinction is made between "diagnosed" and "non-diagnosed" groups in project populations. The distinction is important, even if it is not always clear-cut, because the choice of target groups for service by a mental health facility reflects its aims. Diagnosed populations may be categorized as mentally ill, alcoholic, or addicted. Another group, adjudged delinquents and/or adult offenders, is added because insofar as their intrapsychic difficulties got them into trouble with the law they resemble the three other groups, and the problems of mental illness and crime frequently lend themselves to similar methods of handling.[4] This is not to imply that adjudged delinquents or adult offenders are necessarily mentally ill, or even exhibit char-

---

[4] "Court and Clinics," *Psychiatric Spectator,* Vol. IV, No. 1 (November, 1966). Based on report of field study by Arthur Mathews Jr., *Mental Illness and the Criminal Law,* (Chicago: American Bar Association.)

acter disorders. As a legally adjudicated group, however, they tend to be referred by courts for more psychiatric diagnostic screening than other groups who do not encounter the machinery of criminal law.

Nondiagnosed groups include those selected on the basis of social problems (the underprivileged, school dropouts), vulnerable age groups (infancy, adolescence, old age), or groups without a specific problem focus (union members, college students, the community at large).

Among the diagnosed and nondiagnosed, it will be important to note the distribution of a number of demographic characteristics, for example, sex, age, and ethnic origin.

In discussing the types of care provided by the projects, several different dimensions are relevant: for example, broadly whether the care was in- or outpatient, or the auspices of the care (hospital affiliated or social agency affiliated). Since our focus is on innovations in care, care-systems are organized into the traditional, more conventional types of hospital, clinic, and social agency care versus the newer community reach-out programs. The latter would be characterized by the day and night hospitals, halfway houses, home care, foster family care, and a variety of vocational, social, and educational programs geared to helping the sick return to the community, and the well to remain in the community.

GENERAL FINDINGS

The largest number of projects (108, or 58 percent) served only diagnosed populations. The next largest number of projects (47 or 26 percent) served both diagnosed *and* nondiagnosed groups. The smallest number of projects (30 or 16 percent) served nondiagnosed groups only. Among the 108 projects serving only diagnosed populations, most (82 or 76 percent) served only one group, usually the mentally ill. Among the 47 projects serving both diagnosed and nondiagnosed groups, a fairly prevalent pattern included service to the mentally ill, alcoholics, or delinquents, combined with service to the underprivileged or a particular age group.

Table 3.4 shows that three-fourths of the projects (140 projects) served the mentally ill. Entire neighborhood commu-

Table 3.4. Number of Projects Serving Particular Group

Client Groups	No. of Projects[a]	Percent of 185 Survey Projects
Mentally Ill	140	76
Age Group Problems	40	22
Adjudged Delinquents	33	18
Alcoholics	30	16
"Other" Groups (Community at large, college students, and union workers)	28	15
Underprivileged	25	14
Drug Addicts	14	8
School dropouts	12	6

[a] Duplications are unavoidable since projects often served several groups.

nities constituted the largest single group among the "other group" listing (28 projects). This included isolated rural communities and urban ghetto areas in dire need of mental health and social resources. Other interesting populations served were garment workers, who were given mental health care to help them function on their jobs, and college students in need of guidance to enable them to adjust to the academic world.

58

GROUPS SERVED FOR THE FIRST TIME

Many of the groups just mentioned were served for the first time by the project's sponsoring agency. In all, 78 projects attempted to reach clients whom the sponsoring agency had *not* previously served. Among them were the mentally ill requiring prehospital and posthospital care, addicts, alcoholics, and offenders. Persons suffering chiefly from social deprivation or problems arising from an age crisis (children, adolescents, and the aged) also featured prominently among groups served for the first time by the sponsoring agency.

TOTAL NUMBER RECEIVING SERVICE

Approximately 22,000 patients received service by all projects in a given month. We cannot, of course, conclude that this holds true for every month of the year. Projects tended to give service to individuals and small groups rather than to individuals only. Thirty-eight projects reported that they conducted large community group meetings.

DISTRIBUTION OF PROJECT POPULATIONS

SEX

As shown in Table 3.5, within each client group, except one, the overwhelming majority of projects served both men and women equally. This pattern is broken sharply in three instances—alcoholics and delinquents (predominantly men served), and in "other groups" specified by respondents (serving a majority of women). It appears that when whole communities are served (largest single group in "other group" listing) it is

59

the women who tend to be the major recipients of service. Female heads of households in ghetto areas and teenage unwed mothers account for the predominance of women in this group.

Table 3.5. Project Distribution of Sex of Client Groups

Client Groups	Men[a]	Women[a]	Both	Total No. of Projects
		Number of Projects for Client Groups		
Mentally Ill	15	14	111	140
Alcoholics	10	–	20	30
Drug Addicts	4	2	8	14
Adjudged Delinquents	14	2	17	33
Underprivileged	3	4	18	25
Age Group Problems	6	8	26	40
School Dropouts	2	2	8	12
Other Groups Specified	4	23	1	28

[a] Respondents were asked to indicate whichever sex constituted the majority of a given client-group.

AGE

For the entire project population, adults were served by 140 projects, adolescents by 71, and children by 58.

In projects serving the mentally ill, alcoholics, and drug addicts, the majority are adults. As one would expect, projects serving adjudged delinquents and school dropouts are serving adolescents mainly (see Table 3.6). The "under-privileged" client groups fall into several different age groups. An unusual finding is that not one project serving the "underprivileged" spe-

Table 3.6. Major Age Ranges of Client Groups Served in
185 NIMH Sponsored Projects[*]

Age Ranges

Client Groups	Birth to 5 years	6-11 years	12-17 years	18-64 years	65 and over	Multiple Age Groups[a]
Mentally Ill	1	11	11	70	5	40
Alcoholics				20	1	8
Drug Addicts			1	11		2
Adjudged Delinquents		2	12	9		10
Underprivileged	2	2	3	4		14
Age Group Problems	2	4	8	2	13	12
School Dropouts			7			4
Age Groups Specified				6	1	21
Total No. of Projects	5	19	42	122	20	111

[*] Figures indicate the number of projects reporting that the given client-group served a majority in the listed age range(s).

[a] Where several age ranges were served equally, the most common combinations were 6 to 17 years; 18-65 and over; birth to 65 and over.

cialized in the care of the over-65 age group as a separate entity. One would think that this highly vulnerable group (the aged poor) would be selected for more attention.

EDUCATION

Table 3.7 gives the project distribution for client groups with varying educational levels. The majority of projects report that their clients in all groups had less than a high school education. This confirms our assumption that the typical patient would tend to be "under-educated" according to current educational standards.

Another fairly large number of projects indicated a spread of clients' educational levels ranging from less than high school to some college. Only one project, this one serving the mentally ill, reported that the majority attended college.

61

Table 3.7. Major Educational Level of Client Groups Served in
185 NIMH Sponsored Projects*

Client Groups	Less than High School Graduate	High School Graduate	Some College	Less than High School & High School Graduate	Entire[b] Educational Range
Mentally Ill	60	12	1	18	40
Alcoholics	11	4	–	3	8
Drug Addicts	7	–	–	1	5
Adjudged Delinquents	21	–	–	7	4
Underprivileged	21	–	–	1	2
Age Group Problems	30	1	–	4	3
School Dropouts	10	–	–	2	–
Other Groups Specified	10	1	–	1	12
Total No. of Projects	170	18	1	37	74

Educational Level[a]

* Figures indicate the number of projects reporting that the given client-group served a majority in the listed educational range.

[a] Duplications were unavoidable since projects usually served more than one group.

[b] Most projects in this category served clients whose education ranged from less than high school graduate through some college.

ETHNIC COMPOSITION

Table 3.8 gives the project distribution for client groups with diverse ethnic composition. Similar to the findings on nonprofessional staff, the vast majority of projects reported that no one particular ethnic pattern described the majority within the client group(s) which they served. The only exception to this pattern was in the case of service to the underprivileged. Here, 18 out of 25 projects reported that Negroes, Mexicans or Spanish-Americans, and Puerto Ricans predominated, in that order. This finding is highly consistent with other national surveys, which

Table 3.8. Major Ethnic Composition of Client Groups Served in 185 NIMH Sponsored Projects°

Client Group		Ethnic Composition[a]					
	Negro[b]	White Un-classified	Puerto Rican[b]	Mexican & Spanish-American[b]	Re-ligious Groups[c]	Other[d]	Un-known
Mentally Ill	15	18	1	2	7	1	2
Alcoholics	4	5	–	1	–	1	1
Drug Addicts	–	3	1	–	–	–	–
Adjudged Delinquents	8	5	–	2	–	–	1
Underprivileged	5	6	3	4	–	–	–
Age Group Problems	8	7	–	2	2	1	–
School Dropouts	2	1	–	–	–	–	–
Other Groups Specified	4	1	–	–	3	–	1
Total No. of Projects	46	46	5	11	12	3	5

° Figures indicate the number of projects reporting that the given client group served a majority in the listed ethnic group.

a Nationality, race, or religious identification of predominant group served.

b Negro, Puerto-Rican, and Mexican-American clients were classified without regard to religious affiliation.

c Includes Mormons, as well as Catholic, Jewish, and other religious groups.

d Consists of American Indian and Japanese.

report high percentages of these ethnic groups among the poor.[5]

When a particular ethnic group did predominate in any of the other client-groups (that is, the mentally ill, alcoholics, drug addicts, etc.) it was White and Negro which were most frequently reported.

---

5 Report of the National Advisory Commission on Civil Disorders, New York, Bantam Books, March 1968.

OTHER SIGNIFICANT CHARACTERISTICS
OF PROJECT POPULATION

Most frequently reported for all the diverse client-groups was their being poor or "underprivileged." Again this confirms the assumption that the major target population for the NIMH projects would be the mentally ill poor, the educationally disadvantaged poor, and all of the other problem categories mutually interacting with problems of poverty. A few projects serving alcoholics and drug addicts reported that they serve a large middle class group. One project mentions that their specific target group consists of 10- to 12-year-old addicts and potential addicts living in middle class suburbia. However, not one of the 140 projects serving the mentally ill indicates that it is especially concerned with middle class clientele.

Second in importance for the entire project population was some specific degree or type of emotional disturbance. For example, psychosis or schizophrenia were characteristic of the mentally ill patients. In one project, the average length of hospitalization for such patients was 13 years! This type of information is consistent with reports that hospitals are having to cope with increasing numbers of the hard-core psychotic patients as chemotherapeutic advances result in earlier discharge rates for patients with the more hopeful diagnoses.[6]

Many vulnerable age groups being served were also emotionally troubled. One project specialized in children excluded from public schools because of emotional problems. Others were concerned with adolescents and children with language difficulties and emotional adjustment problems. Still other vulnerable

---

[6] Howard A. Rusk, "New Mental Center," The *New York Times,* April 21, 1968, page 58. Based also on NIMH state hospital report data.

groups served were those living in "fatherless families" and aged residents living in low income public housing projects.

TYPES OF CARE GIVEN TO PROJECT POPULATION

For the entire NIMH project population, Table 3.9 gives the numbers of projects which provided the listed types of care. A cursory glance at Table 3.9 shows that inpatient care exceeds any other broad type of care. This is to be expected since the mentally ill constitute the vast majority of groups served. However, a more important finding emerges as one analyzes the inpatient care in terms of whether traditional or newer, more innovative lines are followed. Then it becomes clear that for projects under Hospital Improvement Project Grant Auspices, as well as the more diversified Mental Health Project Auspices, the innovative, community out-reach programs well exceed the traditional inpatient type of care.[7] When hospital care was

Table 3.9. Number of Projects Providing Each Type of Care

Type of Care	No. of Projects
In-patient Care	92
Out-patient Care	73
Day or Night Hospital	32
Halfway House	17
Foster Family Care	16
Home Care	27
Social Agency Care	43
Other Types of Care	53

[7] This data is corroborated partially by a recent report of HIP projects which revealed that at least half of the total HIP projects in the United States have some activity based on the community as a means of providing an alternative to hospitalization or of helping the patient in his efforts to return to the community. *Psychiatric News*, Vol. II, No. 4 (Washington D. C.: American Psychiatric Association, April 1967), page 14.

deemed necessary for a patient, some alternative to traditional hospitalization was provided as a substitute or an important adjunct to the customary hospitalization of the past. A mere 33 projects provided *only* inpatient care, compared with 120 projects providing outpatient clinic care and/or partial hospitalization.[8]

Table 3.10 shows that for the mentally ill, alcoholics, and drug addicts only, inpatient care well exceeds all other types of care. Although this type of care is prominent for delinquents too, comparatively more projects offer outpatient care to delinquents. For the school dropouts, age problem, and other groups, it is the outpatient social agency and "other types of care" which predominate. Study of the content of "other types of care" which predominate reveals that specific educational programs geared to helping the sick to return to the community, and the well to remain in the community, predominate among the types of care not listed in the NIMH survey. In much smaller numbers, but nevertheless significant, are the storefront centers, group housing projects, and one-the-job services provided to help the sick and the general populace to cope with the daily stresses and crises of life.

Since for the underprivileged client groups alone the unlisted "other" type of care exceeded all other care extended, some illustrations are given below.

Particularly exciting was a program of preschool training for poor, culturally deprived children and their families. Two types of nonprofessional staff, teacher aides and home visitors, were employed in this dual-purpose program; the primary goal was to reach underprivileged children in their preschool years and to instill in them new and healthy values intrinsically related to future academic skills which they would hopefully

---

[8] Complete data for this is given in Chapter 7.

Table 3.10. Project Distribution of Type of Care Provided to Client Groups

Client Groups	In-patient	Out-patient	Day or Night Hospital	Half-way House	Foster Family Care	Care In Own Home	Social Agency Care	Other Care Specified
				Types of Care[a]				
Mentally Ill	82	63	29	12	15	21	23	27
Alcoholics	20	18	7	4	1	2	6	4
Drug Addict	10	7	3	3	–	–	2	1
Adjudged Delinquents	11	17	7	7	1	2	6	7
Underprivileged	2	11	4	1	1	3	7	20
Age Group Problem	14	17	3	–	4	8	15	11
School Dropouts	1	7	2	–	1	2	3	1
Other Groups Specified	7	11	1	1	–	4	4	15
Total No. of Projects	147	151	56	28	23	42	63	86

[a] Types of Care were reported along several overlapping dimensions. See text. Also, most projects provided more than one type of care.

develop. Recognizing the cultural rift between parent and child which this type of educational program almost inevitably creates, nonprofessionals were sent into the homes to try to effect a similar evolution in values and attitudes on the part of the parents. The recognition of the significance of parental values in determining a child's success or failure in the academic milieu was a unique contribution of this project. The social distance between parent and home-visitor was considerably less than that which usually prevails between poor parents and professional teachers; this was another significant asset in the conduct of the program.

Other programs of help to the underprivileged included planned parenthood education, specialized vocational aid, and housing aid. These were conducted with a heavy reliance on indigenous nonprofessionals (see Chapter 4).

However, the more unusual types of care programs were by no means limited to the underprivileged. An exciting program of camping as therapy was conducted for the mentally ill, many of whom had spent twenty to thirty years in mental institutions. Campers spent a week in the country, where it was hoped that they would enjoy an atmosphere of permissiveness and freedom, associate more comfortably with each other, assume responsibility for their persons and their belongings, and, finally, contribute more actively in such group concerns as activity planning, upkeep of the lodge, etc. The plan involved the active participation of campers and counselors, with as little distinction as possible between patients and employees.

A relaxed simple schedule prevailed in the camp. In certain activities, patients were required to participate; in others, participation was optional. Everything except medications was kept unlocked, and patients could walk the grounds freely. However, bizarre behavior was discouraged and more realistic modes encouraged through behavioral reinforcement techniques. The nonprofessional "counselors" helped to develop socializing routines to improve the conduct of campers at dining and other times of the day.

Those involved in this experiment found it to be a tremendous success. Much bizarre behavior was eliminated, patients were relaxed, enthusiastic, and acting more responsibly. One complaint voiced was that the group leader-to-patient ratio was too large. It was felt that the program could have been more effectively implemented had the ratio of nonprofessionals to patients been 1:6 as opposed to the actual 1:10. Despite this shortcoming, this program is one example of a somewhat more imaginative approach to helping the chronically mentally ill.

TYPES OF CARE GIVEN FOR THE FIRST TIME

In all, 73 projects gave "new" types of care not previously given by the sponsoring agency. Prominent among new types of care were intensive approaches to rehabilitate the project populations socially, educationally, and vocationally within a milieu geared to changing the traditional "patient" into a "citizen" capable of meeting the demands of life in the community.

THE CHANGING PICTURE IN CARE PROGRAMS

A result of the changing goal in treating the mentally disturbed is that the traditional relationship between structure and function of agency-sponsored projects has broken down. Settlement houses give after-school activity therapy programs for disturbed children in a slum area rather than the usual recreational care. Educational facilities are providing outpatient care to drug addicts. Projects in traditional casework agencies are offering broad community development programs rather than the one-to-one relationship between caseworker and needy client. State hospital projects are providing "industrial therapy" in cooperation with representatives of community business firms and vocational agencies. Thus, the type of setting—hospital, clinic, social agency, school—no longer helps us to predict the types of care which will be provided.

UTILIZATION OF NONPROFESSIONALS

As indicated above, there is a sharp difference between the ratio of utilization of paid nonprofessional staff in community settings as compared with institutional settings. The institutional settings (used mainly for the mentally ill and other diagnosed groups) tended to have medium and high ratios of nonprofessionals to professionals. The opposite is true for community settings (used mainly for nondiagnosed groups), which tend to have low ratios of paid nonprofessionals.

PROJECT GOALS

Most projects were concerned primarily with providing treatment and rehabilitation for chronically and severely ill individuals. Nevertheless, one-fifth of the projects are making efforts to provide for the general community mental health.

Nonprofessionals are not being much utilized in the few projects which focus more exclusively on early location of disturbed individuals. Significantly, in the small number of projects which divide their attentions equally between providing education to the community, searching out new and early cases, and offering comprehensive treatment and rehabilitation programs, the nonprofessionals *are* being utilized for secondary prevention goals. Not only are they being utilized in the service of these goals, but also their contribution is evaluated as "substantial."

Significant relationships were found between predominant planned goals and type of setting, goals, and mental health of project population, etc. High ratios of paid nonprofessionals to professionals were found chiefly in relation to treatment and rehabilitative goals and settings (tertiary level).

PREVENTION AND INNOVATION IN PROJECTS
PREVENTIVE OBJECTIVES AND ACTIVITIES

A new perspective on preventive efforts emerged from the distribution of index scores (see Chapter 7 for discussion on index rationale). Three-fourths of the projects scored medium or high on the preventive index. This is in contrast to the analysis of projects goals, which indicated that the majority had low-level preventive objectives. A major reason for the difference appears to be that many of the projects planning to treat only those who are already severely ill are making substantial efforts to prevent their patients' continued illness by providing alternatives to the usual inpatient care. In addition, they are engaging in activities and types of care aimed at preventing similar illness for others in the community.

The type of project setting, its location, and ratio of use of nonprofessionals, were found to influence project scores on the prevention index. Projects located in the larger cities, in mental health clinic and other community settings, and employing relatively lower ratios of nonprofessionals, tended to have higher preventive index scores than those projects in comparatively smaller cities, and in institutional care settings utilizing higher ratios of nonprofessionals.

71

INNOVATION IN INDIVIDUAL PROJECTS

An index was developed to measure innovation of nonprofessionals in types of care, functions, etc. not previously given by the project's sponsoring agency (refer to Chapter 7). In contrast to the prevention index, which related more to the total mental health field, the innovative index related more to nonprofessional use per se, and specifically to individual projects. It was concerned with first-time use of nonprofessionals, and with attempts to reach "new" groups, to offer "new" types of care, to recruit and train persons not previously considered eligible for careers in the human services field, and more.

Three-fourths of the projects were considered moderately or highly innovative according to our criteria for "innovation." Having nonprofessionals perform functions which sponsoring agencies had not previously provided proved to be the single, most frequently mentioned "innovative" response.

4

CHARACTERISTICS OF THE
NONPROFESSIONAL POPULATION

A considerable amount of literature has been produced in recent years on the characteristics of both paid and volunteer nonprofessionals. However, most of these documents have described specific projects. Our over-all, aggregate view of the characteristics of nonprofessionals employed in mental health programs has been sketchy and impressionistic.

For planning purposes, it is important to know as much as we can about the general characteristics of those who will play an increasingly important role in mental health programs. We need to know who the nonprofessionals are, where they come from, how old they are, what they are employed to do, and so on. Based on responses to the 1968 NIMH Nonprofessional Manpower Study, our view of some of these basic characteristics is more complete. This view provides us with a reliable basis for future studies both for comparison purposes and for deeper probes into particular characteristics. But, equally if not more importantly, we have now an overview which strengthens the assumption that the reservoir of potential nonprofessionals is varied and vast.

This chapter describes the gross but essential characteristics of those involved in the 185 NIMH-sponsored projects in the 1968 Study. The significant characteristics of the nonprofessionals which are selected for attention include salary status (number of paid vs. volunteer workers), staff category (job titles given by projects designating functions such as case aide and nurse's aide), and staff characteristics, which includes sex, age, education, ethnic composition, and "indigenous" characteristics (similarity of social problems and/or background between nonprofessionals and patient-groups).

The statistical data for these characteristics provide a broad description of who the nonprofessionals are. Where appropriate, comments on the implications of these statistics are included. In the following chapter, the tasks carried out by the nonprofessional are described and analyzed. The last section of this chapter contains a brief résumé of a few selected characteristics for eight NIMH projects, each of which employed at least one hundred nonprofessionals. Because these eight projects employed over 40 percent of the total nonprofessional population surveyed, they constitute exceptions from the norm. The characteristics of these projects which tend to distort the over-all picture have therefore been selected and presented separately.

It should be noted also that for salary status, staff category, and sex, results are based on an exact count of the persons employed. For education and ethnicity, estimates of majority characteristics are reported.

SALARY STATUS, SEX, AND STAFF CATEGORY
SALARY STATUS

Among the 185 projects surveyed, slightly more than one-half (96) employed paid nonprofessionals only, in addition to their professional staff. Thirty-five projects (19 percent) utilized volunteers only. Paid nonprofessionals in combination with volunteers were utilized in 54 projects (29 percent). A total of 10,417 nonprofessionals were reported in the 185 projects. These were almost evenly divided between paid staff (5,220) and volunteers (5,197).

SEX AND SALARY STATUS

Females outnumber males in both paid and volunteer categories. There are 5,843 (56 percent) women and 4,574 (44 percent) men. Females constitute 58 percent of the paid staff and 53 percent of the volunteer staff.

The stereotype of the volunteer as an exclusively female, leisure-class phenomena, representing a negligible number of the total work force in mental health is obviously not borne out by this data. Nevertheless, it should not be assumed that there is a complete trend toward employment of a higher proportion of males in all nonprofessional job categories. To illustrate, in 1963 an NIMH survey revealed that 60 percent of the psychiatric ward aides were female. Four years later (in this survey), females account for 72 percent of the psychiatric ward aides.[1] This change probably reflects the effect of a greater reliance on drug therapy and a corresponding diminished need for physical control of mental patients by male aides.

STAFF CATEGORY

Although job titles offer a highly incomplete view of the functions performed by nonprofessionals, the range of titles is impressive and indicates the wide variety of functions performed.

---

[1] It should be noted, however, that these two surveys are not directly comparable. The first-mentioned concerned 96,200 ward aides in 282 state and county mental hospitals in the nation. (Reported in *Highlights from Survey of Psychiatric Aides*, NIMH Publications 12, April 1964, Public Health Service Publication No. 115.)

Five traditional staff categories were listed in the survey questionnaire, and respondents were asked to designate other possible job titles and indicate the number in the prelisted or write-in categories. The results appear in Table 4.1. It should be noted that these titles give only a gross indication of actual tasks, and functions performed often overlap.

Table 4.1. Distribution of Nonprofessional Staff Categories in 185 NIMH-Sponsored Projects

Staff Category[a]	Number of Non-professionals	Percent
Tutor Teacher-Aides	2,267	21.7
Recreation & Groupwork Aides[*]	2,092	20.0
Nursing & Ward Personnel[*]	1,758	16.9
Other Staff Categories[b] [*] (other than listed)	1,122	10.8
Home Visitors-Enablers	1,020	9.8
Case Aides[*]	666	6.4
Physical, Occupational, Vocational Rehabilitation Aides[*]	355	3.4
Neighborhood Community Organizers	293	2.8
Special Skill Instructors	279	2.7
Community Mental Health Aides	268	2.6
Reach-out Aides	185	1.8
Foster Parents	60	0.6
Homemaker[*]	52	0.5
Total Staff	10,417	100.0%
Number of Projects Participating in this Study	185	

[a] Starred categories were prelisted; the other categories were organized from titles supplied by respondents.

[b] Other titles specified included "Teacher-moms," Social Workers without M.S.S. degree, Alcoholics Anonymous, Cadre workers, and Credit Union workers. However, the largest category in "other staff" was that of volunteer clergymen.

The majority of the nonprofessional staff is comprised of tutor teacher aide, recreation and groupwork aide, and nursing and ward personnel. Note, however, that titles supplied by respondents reflect newer and more innovative uses of nonprofessionals. Such innovative uses account for 52 percent of all nonprofessionals.

The actual percentage of nonprofessionals involved in these "innovative" jobs is probably higher than indicated because, although a sizeable number of respondents utilized the prelisted, traditional staff categories, they noted that it was difficult for them to accurately categorize their nonprofessional staff by title. For example, one project concerned with rehabilitation of long-term psychiatric patients categorized its nonprofessional staff as "recreational groupwork aides" but added an illuminating note: "Each group leader was given the responsibility for developing the treatment program most appropriate for his or her group of ten patients. . . . The group leader sometimes functioned as nursing personnel, recreational worker, occupational therapist, vocational counselor, etc." Another example is that of the psychiatric aide activity workers, categorized in some projects as recreation group work aides. These staff members actually performed a combination of nursing and recreational tasks.

Most projects employed more than one staff category. For example, one project, in coined terminology called a "work-reation program," designed to provide a positive mental health experience for adolescent youths through combined employment and supervised recreation during summer months, had seven paid and volunteer staff categories. Among many projects there was a wide variation in the number employed in each staff category. The widest range—one to seventy—was found for nursing personnel in the projects.

COMPARISON OF SEX AND STAFF CATEGORY

In most job categories there are more females than males, but there are a few notable exceptions. The survey indicated that there were almost twice as many male case aides as there were female. However, almost half (200) of these male case aides were in a single project working as university student "models" for public school boys considered to be delinquent-prone.

Another interesting exception to the general pattern appeared in the open-ended staff category, "Other staff categories not listed." Here one finds 807 men and 315 women. This predominantly male group consisted of large numbers of volunteer clergymen (530) and other professionals (for example, lawyers, doctors) whose training was not in the core mental health disciplines.

In one job title, the predominance of women is particularly marked: women outnumber men three to one in the nursing and ward aide categories.

STAFF CATEGORY AND SALARY STATUS

Table 4.2 compares the various staff categories according to whether they were paid or volunteer. The first two staff categories (tutor teacher aide and nursing and ward personnel) are heavily represented by paid staff. Following these is a group of categories in which there is a fairly even division of paid and volunteer staff, including case aide, community mental health worker, and reach-out aide. The volunteer staff is predominant in the categories designated as recreation group work aide, home visitor companion, and "other staff."

A few explanations are essential to conclusions drawn from this table. Although tutors account for the largest number of

Table 4.2. Staff Category and Salary Status of Nonprofessionals[a]

Staff Category	Number of Non-professionals	Percent Paid	Percent Volunteer
Tutor Teacher Aide	2,267	37.1	6.3
Nursing & Ward Personnel	1,758	27.2	6.5
Recreation & Group Work Aide	2,092	8.4	31.9
Case Aide	666	6.6	6.2
Physical, Occupational, Vocational Rehabilitation Aide	355	4.1	2.7
Other Staff Categories not listed[b]	1,122	4.0	17.6
Community Mental Health Aide	268	3.2	2.0
Home Visitor Enabler	1,020	3.0	16.6
Reach-out Aide	185	1.9	1.6
Neighborhood Community Organizer	293	1.8	3.8
Foster Parent	60	1.1	—
Special Skill Instructor	279	1.0	4.4
Homemaker	52	0.6	0.4
Total Staff	10,417	100.0%	100.0%

[a] Arranged in descending order by percent of paid staff.
[b] See Table 4.1 for "other staff."

nonprofessionals, they were employed in a surprisingly small number of projects. A single project in an urban ghetto area hired 1,798 tutors, or almost 80 percent of the total reported throughout the country. In contrast, almost the same number of nursing personnel were more evenly distributed among a greater number of projects. Typically, there were not more than six to eight nursing staff in one project.

Home visitor enablers also tended to have particularly large numbers concentrated in a single project. Apparently, these volunteers tended to be recruited and placed in projects as groups rather than individually. Often, these large groups were students utilized as part of comprehensive demonstration and

79

research programs. An example is the various volunteer high school and college student groups throughout the country organized to provide resocialization experiences for the mentally ill, hospitalized patients.

Historically, the recreation field has been manned chiefly by volunteer nonprofessionals, and supervised primarily by professionals from the fields of education and social work. The high proportion of volunteers among home visitor enablers follows basically the historical pattern established by the nineteenth-century "friendly visitors" in the social work field. In the recent past they became "paid agents" for social agencies, but now, with the influence of the community mental health movement, they have returned in large numbers to a volunteer status.

AGE GROUPS UTILIZED BY PROJECTS

A broad indication of age trends in use of nonprofessionals may be seen in Table 4.3, entitled Major Age Ranges of Nonprofessionals. This section will highlight findings and observations drawn from the NIMH statistical study and from examinations of selected project responses.

Respondents were asked to classify the age of the majority (more than half) of the members of each staff category within their particular project. If two age groups were utilized equally, they were asked to indicate both, that is, under 18 and from 22 to 64. Four age categories were studied in the survey: 1) under 18 (adolescents); 2) 18-21 (young adults); 3) 22-64 (adults); and 4) 65 and over (senior citizens). Some projects employed persons in all of these age ranges.

In general, the nonprofessional staff, whether paid or volunteer, is composed of adults 22 to 64 years of age. The second

Table 4.3. Major Age Ranges of Nonprofessionals in 185 NIMH-Sponsored Projects*

Staff Categories	Under 18		18-21		22-64		65 and Over		Combinations[a]		Unknown	
	Pd.	Vol.	Pd.	Vol.	Pd.	Vol.	Pd.	Vol.	Pd.	Vol.	Pd.	Vol.
Case Aides			5	3	19	11			4	2		
Nursing and Ward Personnel			3	1	51	7			12	1		
Recreation and Group Work Aides			10	7	46	32		2	9	13	1	
Homemaker			1	1	9	7			1			
Physical, Occupational, Vocational, Rehabilitation Aide		1	2	4	42	11			6	1	1	
Community Mental Health Aide	2		1	—	5	2			1			
Reach-out Aide	1		1		6	3				1		1
Tutor Teacher Aide	1		4	2	14	12		1	2			
Home Visitor			4	5	1	1	1	1	1	1		
Foster Parent					4				1			
Community Organizer			1		4	7				1		1
Special Skills					8	7				1		
Other Staff Titles	1		1	2	21	17			2	2	1	2
Total No. of Projects	4	1	37	25	230	117	1	4	39	23	3	4

* Figures indicate the number of projects reporting that the given staff category employed a majority in the listed age ranges. (Duplicated count was unavoidable.)

[a] In five projects persons under eighteen worked in combination with staff of other age groups; in sixteen projects persons over sixty-five worked with staff of other age groups.

largest age group employed by the projects are young adults 18 to 21. Adolescents and those over 65 years of age are utilized to a limited extent.

Not surprisingly, adults are employed in all staff categories. Young adults are employed mainly as community mental health aides or recreation and group work aides. The latter job usually requires physical activity which is more natural with younger persons.

Only twenty-one projects employ the aged, and ten projects employ adolescents. Considering the disparity between this limited utilization and the increasing proportion of these two age groups in the population, it is important to look more closely at those projects which have used these groups. The utilization pattern of adolescents and senior citizens is described below to reveal in what capacity and with what success they were employed.

PROJECTS EMPLOYING ADOLESCENTS

The considerable number of publications relating to the use of adolescents, particularly high school dropouts, suggested that there would be substantially more utilization of this age group than was indicated by the NIMH Study.[2] The pattern of use of adolescents is in many ways similar to that of the young adult group. Although titles for adolescents tended to be limited to recreation and community mental health aide, a reasonably wide range of caretaking, tutoring, and social-therapeutic functions is performed by adolescents in projects geared to neigh-

---

[2] Publications and reports of the Institute for Youth Studies, Howard University, J. R. Fishman, W. L. Klein, B. W. MacLennan, L. Mitchell, A. Pearl, and W. Walker, *Training for New Careers* (Washington, D.C.: President's Committee on Juvenile Delinquency and Youth Crime, 1965).

borhood improvement, treatment, and rehabilitation of the mentally ill.

One interesting use of adolescents was found in a project concerned with milieu treatment of older mental patients. The youthful workers were effective in teaching home management and personal adjustment skills needed by the elderly mental patient after leaving the institution and returning to normal home life. Through the enthusiastic concern of their youthful "occupation therapy" helpers, the aged, chronic mental patients began to recall some of the ways of the outside world to which they need to adapt after a lengthy banishment from the community.

Other uses of teenagers involve the conscious juxtaposition of self-help and career opportunities in the human services for high school students or dropouts with desperately needed service to disadvantaged groups. One well-publicized example of such use was the Homework Helper Program, organized under the Mobilization for Youth Program on New York City's Lower East Side. In this project, public high school boys and girls tutored younger neighborhood elementary school children with learning problems. In the process of helping the younger students improve their reading ability, these adolescent tutors improved their own academic achievement levels. Two factors credited with the success of the program were the offering of "teacher" status to the teenagers and shared background between "teacher" and student, leading to greater rapport than that which usually exists between professional teacher and student living in an urban ghetto.

Two other projects employed adolescent community mental health aides. One project was staffed by Negro youths in a Rochester, New York, public school, the other by Mexican youths in Utah and Wyoming. The latter project employed 16-

to 18-year-old Mexican students in mental hospitals with the hope of interesting them in mental health careers. In both projects, the youths performed a variety of functions, such as tutoring and activity group therapy, in addition to fulfilling companionship roles with school children and mentally ill adults.

A number of publications relating to the specific problems of training teenage "human service aides" have emanated from a project at Howard University concerned with training local youth as mental health aides. Continuing efforts have been made to employ high school dropouts as youth leaders in community-based mental health centers for children and adolescents.[3] Since 1964 teenagers have been successfully trained to serve as aides in a variety of settings such as recreation centers and preschool and day-care centers in Washington, D.C. The use of such aides is new and relatively untried. The difficulties of dealing with adolescents are compounded by the necessity to handle impulsive behaviors by the professional charged with the dual responsibility of training and service to the community.

Historically, child labor legislation was enacted to reduce the numbers of working children and teenagers. State and local Civil Service regulations have continued, particularly during the Depression era, to restrict employment of young people. Forty percent of the NIMH study projects are in state mental hospitals and are therefore subject to these regulations.[4] (It seems ironic that measures once designed to protect the young from exploitation now serve partially to exclude them from useful employment.) One way to increase the total potential manpower supply for mental health programs is to reach younger age groups and to encourage them to explore human service careers before they have entered the labor market or made formal educational plans.

---

[3] *Ibid.*

[4] See Chapter 8 on terminated project outcomes for very recent changes being effected in Civil Service age criteria.

PROJECTS EMPLOYING THE AGED

Only one of the twenty-one projects utilizing persons over 65 made a specific attempt to hire individuals who were aged. Although the sample of aged nonprofessionals is much too small to warrant any statistical inference, study in depth of the projects' experiences suggests that this group is a vast untapped manpower resource in mental health.

Praise was almost unanimous for the aged who were employed in the NIMH projects. For this group, which has suffered a drastic curtailment of employment and income at age 65, the Social Security system has offered little economic incentive to continue working. It is not surprising to find that many in this age group, banished to a life of idleness and monotony, respond eagerly to calls for volunteers; most of the over-65 group are volunteers. As case aides, home visitors, rehabilitation aides, tutors, and even recreation aides, the senior citizens offered the same wide variety of services presented by younger age groups. Many of this group, who offer their services without remuneration, appear to be of a higher educational level than the average nonprofessional. All of the projects indicate that the service rendered by these volunteers justifies the expenses involved in their training. This is an important finding for it is a forceful reply to the skeptics who question whether it is worthwhile to spend time training people over 65.

There are a number of interesting roles for senior citizens. Several projects found this group's long life-time experience valuable in finding and assessing new resources in the community, particularly in locating homes for mental patients. Paid "enablers", some of whom live-in and others who visit, help state hospitals in locating homes for hospitalized chronic patients. In one project, a specific attempt was made to recruit low income, retired homeowners, both Negro and white, to help rehabilitate patients in homes in the community. Caretaking roles would obviously be well-suited to the experience and life-style of this age group; paid houseparent, foster grandparents and other similar titles attest to the prominence of these roles. Participation in beautification of the community and the newer therapies such as milieu therapy is also open to senior citizens. In one project, mentioned above, the aged were trained side by side with teenagers and young adults in the use of the hospital milieu as a treatment tool.

It would seem logical that the aged could be used to help other aged persons, particularly those with shared social background. There is no reason, however, to limit them to work with the aged. One project which utilizes an aged volunteer as a tutor serves adolescents solely. Another project utilizes foster grandparents (a role growing in importance for the aged) as a means of meeting mutual needs of the older and younger persons. The needs of neglected or disturbed children within institutions or in foster homes can often be met by empathic, competent persons over 65. Particularly in the retired group one often finds the qualities of patience, warmth, and interest, regretfully lacking in many adults under 65 who are struggling with pressures of the work-a-day world.

EDUCATIONAL LEVELS

This section describes the education levels of the nonprofessional staff utilized by the NIMH projects. Table 4.4, "Major Educational Levels of Nonprofessionals," summarizes those findings. Four educational categories were studied in the survey: 1) less than high school; 2) some high school; 3) high school graduate; and 4) some college.

Table 4.4. Major Educational Level of Nonprofessionals* in 185 NIMH Sponsored Projects

Staff Category	Educational Level[a]									
	Less than High School Graduate[b]		High School Graduate		Some College		High School Graduate & Some College		Unknown	
	Paid	Vol.	Paid	Vol.	Paid	Vol.	Paid	Vol.	Paid	Vol.
Case Aide	3	1	8	3	13	7	4	4		1
Nursing and Ward Personnel	24	2	21		9	3	8	3	1	1
Recreation & Group Work Aide	12	13	21	10	25	19	7	7	1	5
Homemaker	5	1	4	3	1	2	1	2		
Physical, Occupational. and Vocational Rehab.	5	3	18	4	13	7	13	2	2	1
Community Mental Health Aide	3		1	1	3		1	1		
Reach-out Aide	2	2	2		2	2	1			
Tutor Teacher Aide	3	1	1		13	12	3	2		
Home Visitor	1	2		1	6	5				
Foster Parent	2		3							
Community Organizer	3	3	1	1		1	1	3		1
Special Skills Instructor	1	1	4		2	4	1	1		2
Other Staff Titles	6	4	2		19	8	1	7	2	3
Total No. of Projects	70	33	86	23	106	70	41	32	6	4

* Figures indicate the number of projects reporting that the given staff category employed a majority in the listed educational group.

[a] Duplications were unavoidable since projects utilizing *both* paid and volunteer staff were counted independently.

[b] Combines the categories "did not attend high school" and "some high school." The larger of the two groups was "some high school."

DISTRIBUTION BY EDUCATIONAL LEVEL

The entire gamut of educational levels is represented in the 185 projects surveyed. A sizeable number of projects used people with less than high school education working side by side with nonprofessionals who have some college. The majority of projects within *all* staff categories employed nonprofessionals who were at least high school graduates with or without some college. Approximately one-third of the projects utilized staff who did not graduate from high school. Case aides, recreation workers, occupational therapist aides, and tutors tend to be relatively highly educated. However, most of the other staff categories, in particular, nursing and ward personnel, reveal a more even distribution between high and low educational levels. The lowest educational category (those who did not begin high school) is represented least in the projects.

Certain trends are suggested by the above findings when they are compared with previous surveys and reports dealing with the educational background of selected nonprofessional staff. Surveys of psychiatric ward aides have indicated that only 9 percent of their staff have had some college and the majority of them are not high school graduates.[5] The current concept of the "psychiatric technician"—a college student who spends six to twelve months in hospitals gaining field experience for continued work in the social sciences—appears to be reflected in the study projects as a way of upgrading the universally low educational level which formerly characterized the job of psychiatric aide. Also reflected is the effect of recent federal legislation geared to help persons in high school to complete their education by training for needed nonprofessional hospital occu-

---

[5] *Highlights from Survey of Psychiatric Aides,* See footnote 1 in this chapter.

pations.[6] The trend toward higher education levels for psychiatric aides appears to be established.

A reverse trend would appear to be needed in dealing with shortages of case aide personnel. Having "only a bachelor's degree" has long been considered the mark of the nonprofessional social worker or case aide. But now the Department of Social Services of New York City has opened its doors to less than high school educated case aides (preferably former welfare recipients). This trend is reflected in several projects in the survey. To alleviate manpower shortages, nonprofessionals will need to be recruited from groups within the low educational levels as well as the high.

Because the "new nonprofessional" is expected to tap reserves of low educational groups, projects offering opportunities for persons with limited educational background were singled out for separate study. One group, that of the high school dropouts, has been discussed above. To gain further insight into this issue, twenty-nine projects which hired persons with less than high school education were examined to see what the potential contribution of this group might be.

PROJECTS HIRING PERSONS WHO DID NOT ATTEND HIGH SCHOOL

Only twenty projects (11 percent) hired *paid* nonprofessionals with less than high school education; nine projects utilized these persons as volunteers. Under-educated persons were utilized in both traditional and innovative jobs. They performed a range of functions similar to the more educated nonprofessionals, with somewhat heavier emphasis on case findings, reception, and

---

[6] Manpower Development and Training Act (1962), Vocational Education Act. (1963), etc.

caretaking functions. Their ages ranged from under 18 through over 65. The majority of this group belonged to an ethnic minority, for example, Puerto Rican, Negro, or Mexican.

Some of the most innovative jobs were undertaken by the least educated group. For example, both "cadre workers" and "resident probationers" are former drug addicts working in quasi-military settings which are designed to recondition them to the realities of their sickness and the problems of adjustment in the outside world. In one project, garment worker unions and their business agents act as liaison with mental health professionals, spot incipient cases of emotional disturbance, and offer on-the-job therapeutic assistance and help in planning outside care. In one large ghetto, "credit union" workers organize and administer low rate loan programs to protect the poor from continued victimization by local loan sharks. Through a local settlement house program, headed by a clergyman, they intervene in the daily lives of their neighbors, offering help with the crises of life. The relatively newer role of medical expediter and "catalyst" in group situations seems to be particularly compatible for the less educated nonprofessional with his ability to communicate in the language of patients with shared socioeconomic background.

Often, the personality of the undereducated nonprofessional, his empathy for others, and his potential for commitment are more important characteristics than a high level of formal education. With compassion and commitment, the undereducated can be trained within the projects; without these basic traits, formal education often is of little use.

ETHNIC COMPOSITION OF NONPROFESSIONALS

Since America is a melting pot of people of diverse ethnic origins, one would not be surprised to find that the majority of

Table 4.5. Major Ethnic Composition of Nonprofessional Staff in 185 NIMH-Sponsored Projects°

Staff Category	Negro[a] Pd.	Negro[a] Vol.	White (unclassified) Pd.	White (unclassified) Vol.	Puerto Rican[a] Pd.	Puerto Rican[a] Vol.	Mexican-American[a] Pd.	Mexican-American[a] Vol.	Religious Groups[b] Pd.	Religious Groups[b] Vol.	Other[c] Pd.	Other[c] Vol.	Unknown Pd.	Unknown Vol.
Case Aide	4	1	7	2					2	1	1	1	2	
Nursing & Ward Aide	5	2	10	4					2		5		1	
Recreation & Group Work Aide	4		19	10	1		1	2						
Homemaker	1		2	3					1	2	1	1	1	
Physical, Occupational, Vocational Rehab. Aide	3		8	4									3	
Community Mental Health Aide	2		1	1	1		1				1			
Reach-out Aide				1	1			1						
Tutor Teacher Aide	4	1	4	1			2			1		1		
Home Visitor	2		1	5										
Foster Parent	1													
Community Organizer	1			2	2	1						1	1	1
Special Skills Organ.	2		1	2							1		1	1
Other Staff Titles	5		3	4	2	1				1	4	1	1	1
Total No. of Projects	34	4	56	39	7	2	4	3	5	5	13	5	9	3

° Figures indicate the number of projects reporting that the given staff category employed a majority in the listed ethnic group.

a Negro, Puerto Rican, and Mexican-American staff were classified without regard to religion.

b Refers to group exclusively related to religious sect.

c Hawaiian (and combinations of two or more ethnic groups) represented here.

projects reflect this heterogeneity. (See Table 4.5, "Major Ethnic Composition of Nonprofessional Staff Categories in 185 NIMH-Sponsored Projects.") Yet, there is an interest in ascertaining whether the ethnic minorities—Negro, Puerto Rican, Mexican, Indian—are represented within the nonprofessional staff of our projects, and in which job categories.

Our awareness of proportionately higher unemployment of ethnic minority groups stimulated concern with this issue.[7] Since minority groups are not evenly distributed throughout the country, it is not surprising to see that most projects hiring large numbers of Negroes, for example, were located in the central cities of Washington, D.C., New York, and Chicago—cities which have higher proportions of Negro population than exists for the nation at large. Similarly, Mexican-Americans are employed in projects in New Mexico, Texas, California, and Wyoming.

Although white personnel predominate in both paid and volunteer mental health jobs, Negroes constitute the ethnic group second most represented among paid workers. Thirty-four projects employed predominantly Negro paid staff, compared with the fifty-six projects employing a majority of paid whites. Many projects hiring nursing and ward personnel, tutors, and case aides reported that their staff was predominantly Negro. Considering that several of these projects were among the eight which employed more than 100 persons in a particular staff title, the actual number of Negroes employed is probably fairly large.[8] Clearly, the proportion of Negro teacher, psychiatric, and case aides is higher than their proportion in the country at large.

Negroes were identified as predominant as volunteers, however, in only a few projects. These tended to be older persons,

---

[7] *Report of the National Advisory Commission on Civil Disorders* (New York: Bantam Books, 1968), pp. 392, 402.

[8] Refer to Chapter 3, section entitled "Projects Hiring More than 100 Persons."

such as retired Negro home owners who located homes in the community for mentally ill patients. Since United States Negroes are over-represented in the lower socioeconomic strata, we would expect that they should seek paid rather than volunteer employment.

Within the Negro retired group and growing middle class, more active recruitment of volunteers might well be productive. Participating in mental health activities might help the volunteer Negro to enter community affairs and to become a more integral part of American community life.

The following section on indigenous workers further describes the use of minority ethnic groups.

"INDIGENOUS" GROUPS

Although the dictionary defines indigenous as "native to or residing in a certain locality," recent usage has expanded the term's meaning beyond geographic reference. Indigenous workers were classified in the NIMH study along two dimensions: (1) similarity of problem or illness between staff and client group; and (2) similarity of socioeconomic characteristics—for example, living in the same slum area, or belonging to the same income or ethnic group. The prime focus in this inquiry was on those in the former classification, that is, the former mental patients, drug addicts, delinquents, alcoholics, etc., since so many of the study projects are designed to help client groups with these problems.

GENERAL FINDINGS

One quarter of the projects (41) utilized paid nonprofessionals who had problems similar to the patient (client) group. One-sixth of the projects (27) had volunteer workers with problems similar to the patient/client group. And in one-third of the projects (68), nonprofessionals, both paid and volunteer, lived in the same neighborhood or belonged to the same social class or ethnic group as the clients. Yet, only 42 projects attempted to hire persons with such characteristics. Some of the social characteristics common to both nonprofessionals and client/patient groups were work experience, age, culture, ethnic background, religious affiliation, and language spoken (other than English).

ILLUSTRATIONS

Certainly the concept of indigenity is not totally new to the mental health field, but the extent of focus on this issue in the utilization of nonprofessionals warrants presentation of a few illustrations.

In one neighborhood program in Texas, Mexican Americans, many of them young adults and former "delinquents," counseled others of their ethnic group who were school dropouts or delinquents. Guidance was given also to the parents of the client group by other middle-aged Mexican-Americans who had wrestled with similar problems that they encountered in their own children.

In the Williamsburg section of Brooklyn, (a depressed community composed of 60 percent Puerto Ricans, 25 percent Hassidic Jews, and 15 percent Negroes), residents organized a program which was geared to improve their own lives and the lives of their neighbors. Plans for a housing development were formulated. Credit unions and counseling and recreation programs were created. The purpose of the project was to involve deprived persons, particularly the youth in the area, in creating programs with meaning for them as individuals and for the betterment of the entire community. The assumption underlying this settlement house project is that there are untapped human capabilities in this underprivileged neighborhood. If leadership potential and native ability are skillfully developed, residents become nonprofessional workers, building their own community beyond the confines of their formerly isolated ethnic enclaves.

PROJECTS UTILIZING 100 OR MORE NONPROFESSIONAL PERSONNEL

Eight projects (out of a total 185) hired unusually large numbers of nonprofessionals. For most of the statistical results, the magnitude of these projects did not significantly deviate from the typical project. The responses to three questions, however, were sufficiently different to justify a separate extrapolation. Short summaries of these results appear below.

1. *How many nonprofessionals were involved in these eight projects?* Of the total nonprofessional staff reported in this study (10,415), over forty percent (4,668) were reported by the eight large projects. The ratios comparing nonprofessionals and professionals in these eight projects, as opposed to the other projects surveyed, are shown in Table 4.6.

Table 4.6. Ratios of Nonprofessionals to Professionals

Ratio	All Projects	8 Large Projects
Nonprofessionals to Professionals	6:1	75:1
Nonprofessional Work Hours to Professional Work Hours	8:1	753:1

2. *Where were these eight projects located (Rural vs. Urban)?* Half of the eight large projects were located in medium-sized cities (25,000 to 499,999), three were in cities over 500,000 population, and one was situated in a rural area (less than

2,500). That even one project involving such large numbers of persons is located in a rural area is surprising. Particularly interesting is the fact that although transportation to this project (located in an isolated rural area) was listed as a problem in recruiting personnel, over 400 nursing aides (and several community home aides) were recruited for an innovative geriatrics program. Elderly persons were screened so that the hospital would not be used as a dumping ground for their care. Appropriate homes in the surrounding rural areas were found. For those who truly needed mental hospital care, early and intensive rehabilitation was instituted to facilitate the patient's return to the community following hospital treatment.

3. *In what capacity did these projects hire nonprofessionals?* These projects hired both men and women, paid and volunteer workers, as case aides, tutors, recreation and group work aides, nurse's aides, companions, and clergymen. One project alone hired 1,798 tutors, all of whom were high school students.

CONCLUSION

Tremendous human resources for mental health service obviously exist. Men and women in a wide variety of paid and volunteer staff categories are performing traditional and innovative jobs to a degree that destroys many of our old stereotypes about who are our volunteers, our paid workers, etc. The least educated are doing some of the most innovative jobs reported. Some projects experimented with the utilization of extremely large numbers of nonprofessionals.

5

FUNCTIONS* PERFORMED BY NONPROFESSIONAL AND PROFESSIONAL STAFF

INTRODUCTION

Quite disparate opinions have been confidently expressed about the impact of nonprofessionals in mental health work. These have ranged from the claim that nonprofessionals are taking over most of the professionals' tasks to the other extreme that nonprofessionals are only being given the most routine, menial tasks which professionals wish to be rid of anyhow.

There is no evidence to support either extreme contention. Rather, as will be described in this chapter, nonprofessionals, to a highly significant degree, are engaged in new roles and functions not previously performed by either professionals or nonprofessionals. And, many of these roles are therapeutic in nature.

As recently as 1963, the Survey of Psychiatric Aides[1] found that 90 percent of the duties performed by this group of nonprofessionals were menial and routine, involving little which could be called psychotherapeutic.

---

* The terms function and task are used interchangeably.

[1] *Highlights of Survey of Psychiatric Aides,* see footnote 1, Chapter 4.

An extremely wide range of functions was discovered being performed by nonprofessional staff in the 1968 NIMH Projects Study. In the majority of projects, nonprofessionals are performing highly innovative functions; that is, functions not previously performed by the project's sponsoring agency. There is evidence of a breakdown of the traditional divisions of functions by nonprofessional mental health disciplines. Case aides, nursing and ward personnel, group work aides, community mental health aides, tutors, and many others are performing practically all functions from case finding to community improvement. The newer social relationship therapies for individuals and groups exceed the performance of all other functions by nonprofessionals.

Although professionals and nonprofessionals alike are working together on most of these tasks, there is clear evidence of differential performance of certain functions. The responsibility for teaching nonprofessionals, as well as training and supervising them in the diagnostic and dynamic knowledge for "screening" and therapeutic functions, rests clearly on the shoulders of the professionals.

This study does not evaluate systematically how well nonprofessionals are performing all of their tasks, although we have some comments of project directors, and unsolicited reports from many of the NIMH projects relating to this issue. Nor is it possible to give a quantitative assessment of the amount of time spent on the various functions (old and new) performed. But substantial data have been collected on the nature of the tasks being carried out by thirteen nonprofessional staff types (either paid or volunteer) and the different functions performed by nonprofessionals in the eighteen tasks listed in the questionnaire.[2]

The major questions concerning functions include the fol-

---

[2] See Appendix A, Questionnaire, page 195.

lowing: What is the range of tasks being performed by non-professional staff in the NIMH projects? Are nonprofessionals performing traditional therapeutic functions which were previously considered the prerogative of the trained professional (for example, individual counseling)? Or, are they performing the newer "social therapies" (for example, resocialization, milieu therapy) based on the combined chemotherapeutic and community care revolution in the care of the mentally ill?

Which tasks are performed most and which are least emphasized? Which categories of nonprofessional staff are performing the above tasks? What is the differential distribution of functions along professional-nonprofessional lines in the projects? Which tasks are performed equally by nonprofessionals, mainly by nonprofessionals, mainly by professionals, etc.? Are any "specialized" techniques being used by nonprofessionals in the service of performing their mental health tasks? Can we discern any significant relationships between the functions performed by nonprofessionals and the type of project setting, geographic location of setting, or other considerations?

FUNCTION ANALYSIS

For purposes of analysis, the functions listed in Table 5.1 are organized into three major categories as follows:

1.) *Therapeutic Functions*: this includes individual counseling, group counseling, socializing relationships, activity group therapy, milieu therapy, and other therapeutic functions.

2.) *Special Skill Functions*: this includes tutoring, various types of retraining, and other special skills.

3.) *Community Adjustment Functions*: this includes job and home finding, facilitating access to community services, and other means of adjustment.

In addition to these major categories, the following five

specific functions are listed: (1) case finding and facilitation of access to project services; (2) reception orientation to service; (3) screening (nonclerical) referring to assessment of suitability of patients/clients for service offered; (4) caretaking (for example, ward care and day care); and (5) community improvement. In this way, an entire range of preventive and therapeutic functions is listed.

Broadly, therapeutic functions lead the list of major categories of tasks carried out in most of the NIMH projects in which nonprofessionals are utilized. Table 5.1 presents the project distribution of the three major categories, followed by the five specific functions which have been listed.

Among therapeutic functions, the newer social relationship therapy[3] for individuals and groups, which is performed in 74 percent of the NIMH projects, exceeds the performance of all other therapeutic functions. Individual counseling, group counseling, and milieu therapy (other therapeutic functions) were performed by nearly one-half of the projects.

In contrast, the least performed function was community improvement (13 percent of the projects). These figures attest to a wide range of functions performed in the NIMH projects as a whole. What is not shown in Table 5.1, however, is the remarkable breakdown of traditional divisions of function by nonprofessionals associated with each of the professional disciplines.

One might expect that the case aide, an outgrowth of professional social work, would concentrate most heavily on case finding, resource finding, and the therapeutic functions for which most social workers are trained. For nursing and psychiatric ward attendants, closely associated with professional nurses, we would expect the caretaking function to dominate.

---

[3] Defined as companionship and resocialization service functions.

100

Table 5.1. Number of Projects in which Given Functions
Are Performed

Listed Functions	No. of Projects (N = 185)	Percent of 185 Projects
Therapeutic	161	87
Special Skills	125	68
Adjustment to Community	100	54
Casefinding	62	34
Reception	85	46
Screening	62	34
Caretaking	109	59
Community Improvement	24	13

Instead, case aides, nursing and ward personnel, recreation and group work aides, community mental health aides, tutors, and many others are performing practically all of the listed functions from case finding to community improvement.

Nonprofessional staff are performing their newer functions in almost as many projects as they do their traditional tasks. Nursing and ward personnel, for example, develop socializing relationships with patients (individually and in groups) in 48 projects while they perform their usual ward care functions in 49 projects. Physical therapists, occupational therapists, and vocational therapy aides perform individual counseling and activity group and socializing therapies in just about the same number of projects as they do their traditional retraining tasks. For most categories of staff, there is very little distinction of function along paid versus volunteer lines.

The case finding function is done by all staff types with the exception of special skill workers and foster parents.[4]

---

[4] Since foster parents function in their own homes rather than in the usual work setting, their situation is exceptional and will therefore not be mentioned in discussion of each function.

Individual counseling is performed by every paid group except for community organizers and "reach-out aides". Tutoring is done by most staff types. Caretaking, which we would expect to be performed by nursing and ward personnel, homemakers, foster parents, and to a limited extent by case aides, is being done in a significant number of projects by physical, occupational therapy aides, group work aides, and many others.

LINK BETWEEN SPECIAL TITLES AND FUNCTIONS

As indicated in Chapter 4, there are certain job titles which do offer a strong clue to the combinations of functions, old and new, performed in the NIMH projects. "Institutional counselors," "live-in vocational counselors," and "residential group counselors" combine the older custodial ward-care functions with a newer emphasis on vocational retraining, milieu therapy, and group counseling for the mentally ill. "Industrial therapists" perform not only the traditional vocational rehabilitation function but also counseling in personal hygiene, concrete job training, and direct linkage with the industrial community. "Teacher Moms" do more than teach; they provide a needed substitute mother relationship within a learning framework.

"Special reach-out aide" describes the functions of nonprofessional staff called "overture-makers" and "contact-makers" whose major task is to move out into the community to locate groups in need of some type of mental health care, in contrast to those who followed up in providing continued, day-to-day care. The "hospital community representative title also denotes a specialized function. Bridging the gap between hospital and community, this staff kept alert to persons on the verge of mental breakdown so that the crises of recurrent hospitalizations could be handled more quickly and humanely.

DIFFERENTIAL FUNCTIONS PERFORMED BY
NONPROFESSIONALS AND PROFESSIONALS

Are professionals and nonprofessionals performing the same or different functions in the NIMH projects? The implications of this knowledge are extremely important for future educational planning for both groups. If nonprofessionals are expected to continue performing some of the therapeutic functions formerly considered the exclusive prerogative of professionals in mental health, we have an entirely different set of planning guidelines than if sharp divisions of function prevail between the two groups.

We cannot assume that there is no qualitative difference in the performance of a particular function (for example, individual counseling) just because it is performed in the same number of projects by professionals and nonprofessionals alike. It is not within the scope of this chapter to evaluate specifically how well particular tasks are performed, either by nonprofessionals or professionals, or specify what the qualitative differences are in performance of similar tasks.

To understand the differential functions of the two groups, some general background information would help. About one-fifth of the time of all professional disciplines is devoted to the combined activities of training and supervision of nonprofessional staff. Administration of the projects and formal research are other activities which we can assume to have been the responsibility primarily of professional staff.

We are concerned now with the tasks involved in the direct services to patients, clients, and community performed by professionals and nonprofessionals alike. We know that approximately 75 percent of the professionals' time is spent on these direct services, and that almost all of the nonprofessionals' time is devoted to these direct service tasks.

103

Most relevant for the purpose of comparison are the categories of functions performed "mainly by nonprofessionals" versus "those undertaken mainly by professionals." Table 5.2 gives

Table 5.2. Project Distribution Showing Differential
Performance of Functions

Functions	Functions Performed[a] (in 185 Projects)		
	Mainly by Non-Profs.	*Mainly by Profs.*	*Equally By Both*
Caretaking—(e.g., ward care, day care)	37	5	12
Socializing Relationships (Individual or group)	36	17	32
Activity Group Therapy	27	14	21
Tutoring	25	10	6
Milieu Therapy	22	17	20
Facilitate access to Community Services	22	22	13
Individual Counseling	19	35	25
Reception Orientation to Service	18	13	25
Retraining—special skill functions	18	5	4
Resource Finding—home, job	17	22	11
Group Counseling	15	27	24
Other Special Skills	14	3	5
Other Therapeutic Functions	12	2	6
Case Finding & Facilitation of Access to project service	11	17	22
Screening (nonclerical)	11	32	17
Community Improvement	10	11	3

[a] Table is arranged in descending order based on nonprofessional functions.

the data on differential distribution of functions along nonprofessional versus professional lines.

There are some differences as one compares the functions

performed by nonprofessionals to those of professionals.[5] The newer social relationship therapies, which we have already indicated exceed all other task-functions, are much more often performed "mainly" by nonprofessionals than professionals. Tutoring, caretaking, and activity-group therapy also show a clear differential in favor of performance "mainly" by nonprofessionals. On the other hand, screening (nonclerical) is, undoubtedly, performed much more widely by professionals, as with individual and group counseling.

For certain functions, namely case finding and reception, the modal pattern is that of equal performance by both professionals and nonprofessionals. However, there is a sizeable number of projects in which given functions, particularly the therapeutic ones, are performed equally by professionals and nonprofessionals. We cannot, therefore, say that even the socializing relationship function (associated so often with the nonprofessional, home visitor companion) is truly "unique" to the nonprofessional.

A few other implications of this comparative data should be considered at this point. One would expect that the "screening" function, for example, which usually involves considerable diagnostic knowledge and responsibility, would be performed predominantly by professionals. The fact that it is performed at all by nonprofessionals suggests a radical change in attitudes toward the use of nonprofessionals for functions which were previously the exclusive prerogative of professionals. Comments by project directors indicate that the trend is toward much greater sharing of knowledge for use between professionals and nonprofessionals.

---

[5] It should be noted, however, that since this is a survey of nonprofessional utilization, data on the tasks of this personnel was much more systematically sought than that relating to professional performance.

The responsibility for teaching, training, and supervising nonprofessionals in the use of certain types of diagnostic and dynamic material rests on the shoulders of the professionals. Socially important information, intimate knowledge of the patient's day-by-day thoughts and activities, contributes heavily to decisionmaking and planning help for people in need of mental health services.

Nonprofessionals are taking much responsibility in providing the latter type of knowledge, and are absorbing what they need to learn from professionals in order to take on new functions. The manpower crisis provided the original opportunity, but the ability of nonprofessionals to accept the challenge has already changed the traditional dichotomy of professional versus nonprofessional in the performance of mental health functions.

FUNCTIONS PERFORMED FOR THE FIRST TIME BY NONPROFESSIONALS

One-hundred-nine projects reported that their nonprofessionals performed functions which the sponsoring agency had not previously provided. Study of the specific functions performed for the first time reveals that nonprofessionals were not merely filling the gaps created by shortages of professional personnel. Rather, needs for new types of services by new groups of persons were revealed, and the nonprofessional created the task to meet the social need. Again, it is the newer social and educational therapies (companionship therapy, activity group therapy, tutoring, group counseling, and retraining) which lead the list of functions performed by nonprofessionals for the first time in the project sponsoring agency.

Logically, a substantial number of new techniques needed to be learned by nonprofessionals in order for them to engage in

106

these new tasks. A sampling of many of the same "techniques" currently being discussed in professional mental health literature appears in the listing of specialized techniques performed by nonprofessionals. Behavioral modification techniques (including remotivation and reinforcement techniques) are being utilized, particularly in relation to mental illness, drug addiction, and alcoholism. "Reaching out casework" is being stressed in connection with efforts to reach new groups in need of service. Game therapy and family group therapy are also employed. In some projects, efforts are being made constantly to train and upgrade both the nonprofessional and the professional staff and teach them the use of the "milieu" as a treatment tool. Teaching patients in hospitals to improve personal appearance, personal hygiene, and develop good work habits was the responsibility of many nonprofessional staff persons.

Block organization and neighborhood canvassing methods are used by staff engaged in community improvement efforts. Relationships with other agencies are stressed, too, as a technique in community mental health practice. "Alcoholism counseling" is performed by "alcoholism counselors," and "pastoral counseling" is performed by clergymen who volunteer to work with the mentally ill. In one project located on the West Coast, nonprofessionals, along with professionals, are experimenting with several avant garde techniques representing an eclectic blend of therapies from diverse schools of psychiatric and sociological thought.

RELATIONSHIP BETWEEN FUNCTIONS
AND OTHER VARIABLES

It should be obvious that it is difficult to predict which functions will be performed by any given nonprofessional staff worker.

107

Only a few relationships between tasks performed and project goals, settings, or types of population served, emerge as significant. Caretaking, individual and group counseling, and activity, group, and milieu therapy tend to be significantly related to certain settings, chiefly the institutional care settings. The performance of these functions in relation to diagnosed populations (the mentally ill, alcoholics, drug addicts) also well exceeds the margin of chance. Other functions, namely casefinding, reception, special skills, and tutoring, show significance in those projects serving both nondiagnosed and diagnosed types of project population. Certainly, the newer companionship role is performed ubiquitously in relation to all settings and goals of social prevention and psychiatric treatment.

6

RECRUITMENT, TRAINING, AND SUPERVISION OF NONPROFESSIONALS

INTRODUCTION

Since the utilization of nonprofessionals in direct service roles in the mental health field is a relatively new development, such issues as recruitment, training, and supervision have just begun to be explored.

The scope of recruitment is aptly described in a recent California Department of Mental Hygiene publication:

direct application of any technique or effort designed to attract individuals to, or motivate them to enter, a specific area of endeavor . . . or a specific occupation such as psychiatric nursing. The act of recruitment deals essentially with the external aspects of the total problem, with the actions that may be taken by the recruiter to induce the individual in making an occupational choice.[1]

According to George Albee,

we know of no national effort that is consciously, systematically,

---

[1] California Dept. of Mental Hygiene, "Recruitment and Occupational Choice," *Mental Health Manpower, Recruitment, Training and Utilization*, Vol. II (June, 1967) p. 18.

aggressively working at the problem of creating favorable images of professional people among high school students, or even in making certain that all high school students have an opportunity to learn that they are desperately needed in certain fields, such as psychiatry, psychiatric nursing, and psychiatric social work.[2]

The section on recruitment focuses on the methods being directed to various groups, the success of these efforts, and general recruitment problems as they affect study projects.

Training and supervision are primarily concerned with the manner in which the services of nonprofessionals can be made optimally valuable and effective. To the extent that the learning needs of nonprofessionals are understood, programs can be better designed to maximize their potential contribution. In the section on training, approaches are analyzed in terms of whether they were primarily "didactic" or "on-the-job" training. Projects using both methods of practical experience and classroom teaching are also discussed. Last, the section on supervision describes the type of supervision available to nonprofessionals.

RECRUITMENT OF NONPROFESSIONALS

The 1968 NIMH Project Study was designed to gather data which would not only provide a view of the wide spectrum of techniques being employed in the hiring of nonprofessionals but also respondents' evaluations of these techniques in order to make recommendations for more effective hiring practices. Methods employed, effectiveness of each method, problems in recruitment, and attempts to recruit special groups were explored.

---

[2] George W. Albee, *Mental Health Manpower Trends: Manpower for Mental Health,* (Louisville, Kentucky: Kentucky Mental Health Manpower Commission, 1963), p. 5.

It should be noted that recruitment methods, effectiveness, etc. are not compared for each of the various staff categories; instead, these variables are analyzed within the broader groupings of paid and volunteer nonprofessionals.

METHODS USED IN THE RECRUITMENT
OF NONPROFESSIONALS

More than three-fourths of the projects (142) used anywhere from two to seven methods (see Table 6.1). Sixteen percent of the projects (30) used only one recruitment method. The mode was two methods used per project.

Table 6.1 gives the number of projects using different methods of recruitment for paid and volunteer nonprofessional staff.

Table 6.1. Recruitment Methods for Nonprofessional Staff

Recruitment Methods	Paid	Volunteer
Local Employment Agencies	50	
Recommendation by nonprofessionals	53	20
Recommendation by project professionals	68	16
Group Meetings for prospective applicants	18	19
Advertisements in news media, posters	56	9
Talks to community, volunteer, and other groups	18	50
Other	42	10

In recruiting paid nonprofessionals, a number of methods were used. Fewer methods were utilized in recruiting volunteers. Advertisements in news media, recommendation by project professionals, recommendation by project nonprofessionals, and local employment agencies were widely used by projects employing paid workers. The only method frequently used to recruit volunteers was talks to community volunteer and other groups. Infrequently used in hiring nonprofessionals were group meetings for prospective paid workers and advertisements for volunteers in news media.

Other recruitment methods employed for both paid and volunteer nonprofessional staff included contact with colleges, universities, schools of social work, recruitment by word of mouth, use of brochures, state personnel offices, and local poverty and community service agencies.

SPECIAL SCREENING METHODS

Special screening methods were employed by over two-thirds of the projects (124). The use of such methods was more characteristic of paid staff (72 projects) than volunteer staff (17 projects). The single most widely used screening method for all nonprofessional staff was that of individual interviews (38 projects). Thirty-three projects reported using a variety of special screening methods.

One project, for example, which focused on building interpersonal relations with deprived, potential problem children, employed a variety of techniques. In addition to interviews, applicants had to fill out several questionnaires including an adjective check list, a philosophies of human nature questionnaire, a self-disclosure scale, and an introextraversion scale. Since the nonprofessionals in this project were all college students, these techniques could be used successfully for selection purposes. However, with a less literate or less educated group of applicants, a more verbal rather than written self-evaluation process would be needed.

Another project, utilizing undergraduates as child psychotherapists, employed a battery of screening techniques. Applicants were first interviewed by a psychologist who administered a series of tests. Unaware of the psychologist's final verdict, a psychiatrist examined the applicant. Whenever possible, the project hired those persons independently approved by both psychologist and psychiatrist. Certain traits were sought and others rejected in applicants. Rigidity, defined as "the possession of stereotyped attitudes inimical to effective psychotherapy" was counted an undesirable trait. Flexibility, warmth, and spontaneity were desired.

EFFECTIVENESS OF RECRUITMENT METHODS

The method which seemed to have achieved the most widespread popularity and success for recruitment of all nonprofessionals was recommendation by project professionals or nonprofessionals. Not a single project rated either of these methods as not effective. The other methods had a more even distribution among four ratings (very effective, moderately effective, slightly effective, and not effective). In other words, most recruitment techniques were considered to have at least some success whereever they were employed.

PROBLEMS IN RECRUITMENT

Recruitment problems can be grouped in the following major categories: (1) *Situational factors* (include transportation, scheduling of hours); (2) *Personnel arrangements* (salary level, chances for promotion, physical facilities); (3) *Qualifications of the nonprofessionals* (age, sex, education, discomfort regarding problems of project population, difficulties in locating persons with needed skills); and (4) *General lack of response* to recruitment efforts.

More than one-half of the projects in the survey (94) indicated that they had problems in recruiting nonprofessional staff. The single most widespread problem reported as an impediment to hiring paid workers was low wages (52 projects). The over-all problems due to personnel arrangements (that is, little chance of promotion, no reimbursement for work expenses, inadequate physical facilities, as well as low salary) do seem to make it difficult for projects to hire paid staff. There was little evidence, however, that these problems affected the recruitment of volunteers. Recruitment problems resulting from situational factors (for example, transportation to project, scheduling of work hours, etc.) involved those projects hiring paid workers as well as those using volunteers approximately equally.

One project geared to training of practical nurses in the care of the mentally ill highlighted a whole array of recruitment problems resulting from personnel arrangements and situational factors. Among the problems noted were the following: travel distance and time; undesirable shifts; refusal of some hospitals to hire part-time workers; shortage of equipment, supplies, and psychiatrists; frequent changes in shifts which bar long-term association with patients; and too much paperwork.

Another problem of major proportions was defined as the custodial-humanistic conflict. New nurses tended to be humanistically oriented as a result of their recent training, but were subjected to the supervision of those with a more custodial outlook. This factor was considered a major obstacle to the retention of practical nurses.

Problems relating to the qualifications of nonprofessionals (age, sex, etc.) affected primarily the hiring of paid workers, and also had a significant effect in the recruitment of volunteers. Two major problems reported primarily in relation to paid staff were the small number of males applying for jobs and the insufficient education of applicants, even for nonprofessional roles. In regard to the latter, it is to be remembered that "what is

114

sought in the nonprofessional is an ability to communicate and perform at a level that obviates difficulties; not at a level that approaches professional expectations."[3]

The next largest problem indicated was the difficulty of locating persons with needed skills and aptitudes. While this problem was cited mainly in regard to recruiting paid staff, it affected projects utilizing volunteers as well.

Another consideration was the nonprofessional's discomfort regarding the problems and illnesses of the group served by the project. This hindered the hiring of both paid and volunteer staff in a number of projects.

RECRUITMENT PROBLEMS AND LOCATION
OF PROJECT

Smaller cities and towns tended to have more recruitment problems than the larger cities. Residential institutions generally had more difficulty hiring nonprofessional staff than community-based projects. Since the state mental hospital (the major residential institution in this survey) is not infrequently located in isolated rural areas, recruitment problems were compounded for these projects.

ATTEMPTS TO RECRUIT SPECIAL TYPES

Attempts were made by many projects to hire special groups of persons historically under-utilized in the mental health field. Such groups include housewives, college students, and retired people. Another group includes the indigenous personnel—per-

---

[3] Aaron Schmais, *Implementing Non-Professional Programs in Human Services*, Manpower Training Series (New York: Center for the Study of Unemployed Youth, New York University, 1967), p. 43.

sons coming from the same neighborhood, sharing similar social, ethnic, or religious characteristics, or having similar problems or illnesses to those of the client group.

College students were the most sought-after group. More than one-quarter of the projects attempted to hire college students; most of these projects were anxious to hire students on a paid basis. Housewives were the next single largest group projects tried to hire. They were sought equally as volunteers and paid workers. Forty-two projects indicated the intention to hire indigenous nonprofessionals—former addicts, alcoholics, mental patients, high school students, Negro or white youth, and general neighborhood residents. Moreover, these projects were successful beyond their expectations in recruitment of such special persons. Only thirteen projects stated the express aim of hiring retired persons, approximately evenly divided between paid and volunteer workers.

A project concerned with the training of practical nurses in the care of the mentally ill sought to hire individuals who had always wanted to be nurses but had been unable to realize this goal. This was considered an excellent source of nonprofessionals—highly motivated persons who because of practical considerations and a lack of opportunity were never before able to follow desired career lines.

In general, those projects which indicated attempts to recruit "special" types of nonprofessionals specified an interesting array of sought-after individuals. Several projects were anxious to hire teachers and child-care aides. Another group of projects was looking for professionals from other disciplines and those with valuable human service experience. Nurses, physicians, civic officials, and clergymen, as well as nonprofessional social workers, psychologists, employers, and homeowners, were among those listed. Highly motivated members of organizations

116

such as the Girl Scouts, Junior League, Sunday Schools, or sing-
ing groups were also sought. Others, were conscientious objec-
tors, "successful mothers," and persons with potential for professional training. Thus, projects were reaching out to engage and
activate groups and individuals never before considered eligible
for the human services field on such a large scale.

TRAINING OF NONPROFESSIONALS

An understanding of methods employed for training nonprofessionals is of particular importance. An understanding of training
techniques provides some insight into the means whereby nonprofessionals can be made to perform with optimum effectiveness. Training can be defined as the "overall attempt to modify
behavior so that trainees become more capable of performing
tasks. In turn, this is dependent on the acquisition and refinement of skills and knowledge, gaining and deepening insight
and self-understanding."[4]

A finer breakdown is available in our section on training
than on recruitment, since training methods here are related to
staff category as well as the salary variable. The two following
main types of training were studied: (1) didactic courses, lectures, films, and (2) on-job, apprentice training, observation.

Very few projects provide a basically didactic training program for their nonprofessionals of all staff categories. The rule
is for projects to use either on-the-job apprentice-type training
alone or to use this in combination with didactic instruction. The
pattern for paid and volunteer staff is fairly similar. However, a
larger proportion of the paid staff used the combined didactic
and on-the-job approach.

Only a small number of projects offered no training after

---

[4] *Ibid.*, p. 49.

orientation. These, however, tended to apply to only a few staff categories, such as recreation aide, physical, occupational vocational rehabilitation aide, and special skills instructor. One possible explanation for this phenomenon is that nonprofessionals in these categories are often of a high educational level and already trained, thus requiring less formal direction on the job.

SPECIAL TRAINING METHODS

Approximately one-third of the projects employed special training methods. These methods are obviously closely related to the nature of the individual project and the functions of its nonprofessionals. Following are some examples of special training methods:

(a) Project staff workshops, training sessions, or symposiums (7 projects).

(b) Monthly in-service meetings (7 projects).

(c) Weekly staff meetings for all project staff (5 projects).

(d) Daily staff conferences for nonprofessionals (4 projects).

(e) Training during group sessions with patients, nonprofessionals, and professionals present (4 projects).

The daily staff conferences were noted as being a highly effective device to reduce the frustrations faced by volunteers who worked with emotionally disturbed children. For paid nonprofessionals, too, they were found to have a strong morale-building effect which more than offset the investment of the professional's time. Timing a workshop prior to commencement of the project was found to be highly successful in training nonprofessionals and getting nonprofessionals accustomed to working together.

In addition to staff meetings and conferences (both group

118

or individual), it was observed that many projects used special training methods recently made possible through modern technology. Such devices as tape recorders, closed circuit video tapes of patients and therapists, movies, and one-way vision screens were mentioned by a number of projects. These techniques were rarely used alone, but more often in conjunction with a variety of other techniques.

TRAINING IN SPECIALIZED TECHNIQUES

Some projects trained applicants in a variety of specialized techniques. In one project concerned with nurseries in cross-cultural education, teacher assistants were instructed during weekly meetings in "sensitivity" skills, observational techniques, family life education, and specific teaching strategy.

In one study which dealt with mental health aides, training methods based on group interaction and group reinforcement were considered successful in nurturing a sense of identity in nonprofessionals as well as improving ability to communicate with patients and staff.[5] This emphasis on "acting out" instruction appeared to be fairly widespread. Such techniques as role playing, art workshops, field trips, group discussions, and mutual demonstration and criticism sessions were widely reported.

VALUE OF TRAINING

The assumption is often made that nonprofessional status per se ensures greater sympathy to the plight of the client group. However, this is not always so, and the failure to anticipate negative

---

[5] June Jackson Christmas, "Group Methods in Training and Practice: Non-Professional Mental Health Personnel in a Deprived Community," *American Journal of Orthopsychiatry*, Vol. XXXVI, No. 3 (April 1966), pp. 418-19.

attitudes can spell failure for a training program. The fact that the nonprofessional has been hired will often immediately reinforce his social distance from the group being served, and may set off a feeling of superiority, annoyance, or impatience with those he is supposed to help.

A training program will not be successful if it assumes that the nonprofessionals all enjoy being considered representative of the group they serve. Rather, "they will fall into many categories: soft and empathetic, hard and judgmental, others may be manipulative and selfish. . . ."[6]

Thus, the failure to recognize individual personality types on one hand, and the tendency to make overly broad generalizations about nonprofessionals on the other, can lead to a superficial training program. Many project directors are aware of these hazards, and note that the individual character and personality of the nonprofessional was a paramount consideration in training, and that one should not err in generalizing solely on the basis of the nonprofessional's lack of formal mental health training or his "indigeneity."

AVAILABILITY OF SUPERVISION

Because of their limited specialized training prior to job performance, nonprofessionals may be considered as requiring more supervision than do professionals. The question then is, exactly how much supervision was provided for the nonprofessional staff in these projects?

A very distinct pattern emerges regarding the availability of supervision. The large majority of projects hiring nonprofes-

---

[6] Aaron Schmais, *Implementing Non-Professional Programs in Human Services,* Manpower Training Series (New York: Center for the Study of Unemployed Youth, New York University, 1967), p. 50.

sionals, regardless of the staff category, provide them regularly with supervision. A small number of projects provide them occasionally with supervision, and an inconsequential number provide them with supervision only if an emergency arises.

Occasional supervision was provided for two of the staff categories: recreation and group-work aide and physical, occupational, vocational rehabilitation aide. These two staff categories also accounted for a sizeable portion of the group where no training was provided after orientation. This seems to indicate that some nonprofessionals who come to the job with previous instruction can handle themselves with a minimum of training and supervision.

The job title and the nature of the job is also significantly related to the amount of supervision provided. It is not surprising that psychiatric aides, nursing and case aides, community mental health aides, who are almost always intimately responsible for a wide range of caretaking and therapeutic functions, especially in the hospital setting, were held accountable through a system of regular professional supervision within the hospital hierarchical structure.[7]

Chapter 8, which assesses the nonprofessionals' contribution, yields further implications for the training and supervision of nonprofessionals in the context of an evaluation of interaction problems between professionals and nonprofessionals.

---

[7] See A. H. Stanton and M. S. Schwartz, *The Mental Hospital,* for implications of the hospital hierarchical structure for professionals and nonprofessionals alike.

7

RESEARCH FINDINGS IN
PREVENTION AND INNOVATION

Surprisingly little factual or conceptual data is available on goals, despite exhortations on the part of our highest governmental bodies to attend to the critical goals of prevention and rehabilitation in mental illness. Yet, a firm knowledge of goals in mental health projects is essential for rational planning in the mental health field and for developing new models for the use of nonprofessionals.

The theoretical framework used for this analysis of goals is based on an adaptation of the public health model of prevention to the mental health field. As discussed in Chapter 2, a few writers, notably Gerald Caplan, have presented the over-all framework of the following three distinct but related levels of preventive goals.

Primary prevention level: involves specific preventive activities in health promotion (for example, mental health education and anticipatory counseling to would-be mothers, to special age groups—the teenager, the senior citizen about to be retired; homemaker and other service designed to prevent family break-up). All these activities are aimed at reaching people *before* they become mentally ill.

Secondary prevention level: essentially involves locating those who have early symptoms (acute or mild) of mental disorder and reducing the number of serious disorders.

Tertiary prevention level: involves the reduction of the impairment which may result from severe and chronic disorders; usually requires long-term care and rehabilitation.

These three levels are not specifically comparable or independent. Typically, agencies in the community are not organized to deal exclusively with a single level of prevention. Even a program which works with only the most chronically disordered individuals in a state hospital may be offering substantial help at the highest preventive level through individual casework service to family members, educating them as individuals to the facts of mental illness, and making it less likely that they will become ill under the stress of caring for the sick relative. What differentiates this type of service from one belonging to the primary prevention level is that the latter program is directed toward *whole populations* rather than individuals. When a program of primary prevention deals with an individual, he is seen as the representative of his specific population (for example, all young children whose mothers are to be hospitalized for mental illness) and his treatment is planned insofar as he represents a community problem. Specific provision of physical, psychosocial, or cultural supplies is made during crisis or over longer periods of time to alter the balance of forces in favor of a healthier adaptation for a whole population. This kind of plan is expected to increase the probability of escaping mental illness and to improve the ratio of sick to well in the population at large.

Since projects frequently have more than one goal, and

different amounts of emphasis on these goals, combinations of goals were studied in an effort to discern patterns into which each project could be uniquely classified. These patterns, forming a continuum from primary through tertiary prevention, have evolved out of individual case studies in addition to the statistical study. Finally, the typology of goal patterns is ranked and organized into high, moderate, and low preventive goal levels, which are then used to test the statistical significance of goal levels as they relate to other project characteristics and the use of nonprofessional personnel.

QUESTIONS FOR STUDY

The specific questions which we hoped to answer included the following:

1. What are the goals of experimental projects which utilize nonprofessionals in mental health service?

2. Utilizing the public health framework of three preventive levels, how many of the projects have goals which can be labeled as chiefly illustrative of primary, secondary, and tertiary prevention respectively?

3. Is the above concept of preventive levels sufficient in understanding mental health goals or are there other goals in practice which require different concepts?

4. What relationship, if any, is there between the various goal levels?

5. Are the relationships between project goals and other project characteristics (for example, settings) significant?

6. Can we discern different patterns of goals with corresponding patterns of utilization of nonprofessionals?

Despite the broad community preventive concept outlined in the Mental Health Study Act of 1955 (with particular focus

124

on the primary prevention level), and reinforced by subsequent presidential messages since that date, most current preventive mental health work is being done on secondary and tertiary levels; comparatively little is being done on the primary level. This level of prevention has remained the most neglected. The implication of neglecting goals at the primary prevention level must be faced, particularly if one believes that, as we succeed in emphasizing primary prevention goals, the need for secondary and tertiary pathology-focused programs should be substantially reduced. This presupposes a committment to give greater attention to the total community population before its members become ill.

Certain settings (for example, schools, public health facilities, settlement houses, neighborhood service centers and community centers) lend themselves to preventive intervention in the total "normal" community populations before mental health problems are manifest or at least before whole populations are viewed and/or diagnosed in terms of pathology-classification systems. In direct contrast, other settings (mental hospitals, mental hygiene clinics, and rehabilitation centers) deal primarily with the established pathology or "pathological" sub-populations of the community. We would therefore expect that the latter type of agency would be functioning chiefly on the tertiary level of prevention, whereas the former type of agency would tend to function primarily on the primary level of prevention.

Between the two levels would be the settings such as child guidance clinics in schools and community agencies or similar agencies, which are presumed to be geared to case finding, early diagnosis, and prompt treatment. This type of agency would be expected to function chiefly on the secondary level of prevention.

To the extent that a project is found to be dealing with predominantly nonpathological or "normal" client populations, it is expected that it will be characterized as operating at the primary level of prevention. As a project deals with increasingly pathological populations, the project probably will be characterized as operating at the secondary and tertiary levels of prevention, respectively.

One would expect that nonprofessionals will be utilized more fully in dealing with normality rather than pathology. Nonprofessionals, we assume, will more likely carry out the task of educating the general community to improve mental health in contrast to the more strictly clinical activities associated with treatment of already disturbed individuals.

ANALYSIS OF PLANNED GOALS

The complete picture of strongly and moderately emphasized goals, each classified to the appropriate preventive goal level (based on the public health schema), is presented in Table 7.1. It should be noted here that this discussion of goals refers to a project's *planned* goals, as distinguished from those goals which it has *achieved*.

ESSENTIAL OR STRONG GOALS

Several stark facts emerged at this descriptive level. *Three-fourths of the projects reported that providing treatment and rehabilitation to severe and chronically ill and maladjusted groups received their strongest emphasis.* In those projects with only one strong goal (95), the percentage reporting the single strong goal of rehabilitating the severely ill (tertiary prevention) was even higher (82 percent). Contrary to expectations, only 28 percent strongly emphasized the secondary prevention goals of early location, diagnosis, and treatment of suspected or acute

126

Table 7.1. Planned Goal Levels Reported by Projects as
Having Moderate or Strong Emphasis[a]

Planned Project Goal Levels	Strong Goal No.	Percent of Projects Reporting	Moderate Goal No.	Percent[b] of Projects Reporting
Primary Prevention	38	21	19	10
Secondary Prevention	51	28	25	14
Tertiary Prevention	135	73	14	8
Citizen Participation Social Action	37	20	45	24
Other Goals	29	16	7	
Total Reported Goal Levels	290		110	

[a] Since any project may report more than one goal level, the total reported goal levels exceed the number of projects (185). For example, a single project may report both primary prevention and tertiary prevention as strong, or primary prevention as strong and tertiary prevention as moderate, etc.

[b] The base for this percentage is the number of projects (185).

disturbances to ward off the more serious long-term illness and adjustment problems. It should be noted that the Joint Commission on Mental Health recommended that priority be given to prevention starting at the secondary level. These experts were willing to forego priority on the level of primary prevention, but they were keenly aware that failure to plan for identification and treatment of milder disorders could only increase the prevalence of the serious mental disorders in the country.

Why is comparatively little work being done on the secondary prevention level? A partial explanation may be found in study of the data on type of settings and project populations served. Since the mental hospital is the single largest setting in which project patients are served, and since we know that increasingly the population of mental hospitals consists of the hard-core psychotic patient, the goal of secondary prevention logically would not be relevant in this setting. Only one-fifth of the projects focused strongly on promoting and providing for general community mental health (primary prevention). Approximately the same proportion strongly emphasized some form of citizen participation in the life of the community. For example, promoting employment of nonprofessionals, use of volunteers, citizen participation, and social action in the community were the strongly emphasized goals planned, in contrast to a specific mental health service for patients or community.

CITIZEN PARTICIPATION GOAL

Another significant finding is the large number of moderate responses (45) given for the citizen-participation-social action goal. This goal, which can be labeled "citizen participation," rarely appears alone as a strongly emphasized goal.

Study in depth of the 37 projects which focused strongly on citizen participation and social action revealed that many of them offered service considered illustrative of primary prevention; that is, homemaker, housing, and preschool care. Others encouraged citizen participation as a means of developing needed treatment resources for the chronically ill in the community(an example of tertiary prevention). Thus, the citizen participation-social action goals were coordinated with the three major preventive goal responses since they were obviously not on the same level as the three major preventive levels.[1]

DEVELOPMENT OF GOAL PATTERNS

The previous section has discussed goal levels in terms of overall project plans. This approach does not permit classification of a project into a single category which reflects its characteristic

---

[1] The same was true for "other goals"; these were usually specific ways of implementing mental health service which fit into the primary, secondary, or tertiary preventive levels.

goal pattern. In order to discern possible goal patterns into which each project could be uniquely classified, an analysis was made of the combination of goal levels reported as strong. All but ten of the projects could be uniquely classified according to goal combinations. These patterns formed a theoretical continuum from primary prevention through secondary to the tertiary level.

Table 7.2 shows the six goal patterns which emerged. A

Table 7.2. Number of Projects with Six Goal Patterns Based on "Strongly Emphasized" Goals

Goal Pattern	Theoretical Continuum	Project No.	Percent
1	Clearly Primary Prevention	19	10
2	Primary and Secondary	14	8
3	Clearly Secondary Prevention	12	7
4	Secondary and Tertiary	22	12
5	Tertiary	108	58
6	Mixed	10	5
	TOTAL	185 projects	

continuum could be observed of goals representing the primary preventive level, combining with goals at the next level (secondary level), and moving to the tertiary preventive level. As one would expect from findings previously reported, this tertiary group is the largest (58 percent). None of the other goal patterns represent more than 12 percent of the projects.

A very small group of projects (ten) did not fit into the continuum. These reported strong emphases on all three levels or a skip between levels (primary and tertiary). One factor which all of this group had in common was some emphasis on primary prevention. Examples of this small group included the narcotics addiction service centers, which divided their attentions equally between providing education to the community about addiction, searching out early cases of drug addiction (particularly among teenagers), and offering comprehensive treatment programs to established cases of drug addiction. Non-professionals within the centers and out in the community helped here.

The secondary prevention is less easily singled out as an independent level. It sits in the middle, relating to the higher and lower levels of primary and tertiary prevention. Logically, this is as it should be. It deals with influencing the prevalence of mental disorder in a community by early location and prompt treatment; and we know that this can occur in two ways. In one, the rate of new cases can be lowered by altering the factors which led to the disorder (through primary prevention).[2] In the other, the rate of old cases can be lowered by shortening the duration of existing cases through early diagnosis and prompt and effective treatment (classically referred to as secondary prevention).

If more cases of mental disorder are discovered than can be handled therapeutically by existing resources, or if each disorder is not treated early enough before it becomes fixed, clearly the ranks of the severely mentally ill are increased. The relationship to the tertiary level then emerges. The rationale for Goal Patterns 2 and 4 (programs equally focused on primary and secondary prevention, or secondary and tertiary prevention, becomes quite clear.

If we look beyond the numerical data to study the individual projects and their respective goal patterns, several illuminating illustrations and findings appear. These were based on "case" studies of individual projects as a whole rather than a statistical analysis of discrete response items.

---

[2] Prevalence is defined as it is used in public health terminology. It is the rate of established cases of mental disorder at a certain point or period in time. Established cases include both old and new cases of the disorder.

GOAL PATTERN 1: CLEARLY PRIMARY PREVENTION

This group of nineteen projects appears to focus on the broadest and more basic type of community mental health prevention in the entire survey. Planned parenthood programs, services for culturally handicapped children in low-income neighborhoods, and organization of a total community to avoid neighborhood blight are typical of this group.

Most of these programs involve substantial use of volunteers and paid nonprofessionals in community improvement, neighborhood representative, and educational-counseling roles. One program, featuring early school services for culturally handicapped children, concentrated, too, on getting citizens to understand the problems of their fellow clients so that they would vote money to help provide the broad health, welfare, and educational services needed by the poor pupils and their parents in a large disadvantaged area. Another program, geared to preventing complete deterioration of a blighted neighborhood, attempted to involve as many community residents as possible in their fight to save themselves from becoming emotionally demoralized and helpless. It was anticipated that the majority of these programs would be located in community settings, schools, community councils, and settlement houses.

GOAL PATTERN 2: PRIMARY AND SECONDARY PREVENTION

As one would expect, this group of projects involved also a basic type of community mental health prevention, but with the distinction of focusing typically on screening a total school population, and offering such medical and psychiatric services as needed. The projects did not offer treatment; they spotted emotionally or socially disturbed children or high school and college students and referred them outside of the schools to

131

appropriate care. Usually the case finding service was performed by teacher-aides or school advisor aides. In one project, a neighborhood improvement project in a social agency, group work aides located and treated families with many problems.

GOAL PATTERN 3: SECONDARY PREVENTION

Early diagnosis of a special group in need was the typical activity for those projects, indicating a strong secondary preventive goal. This was usually associated with the use of teacher-aides or volunteers with special skills to engage the energies and interests of the troubled group. Public health agencies and child guidance clinics with day hospital programs illustrate this goal pattern. The twelve projects in this group are quite evenly distributed in all the settings, with professional rather than nonprofessional staff responsibility for the case-finding.

GOAL PATTERN 4: SECONDARY AND TERTIARY PREVENTION

Characteristic of this group of twenty-two projects is the presence of treatment resources to cope with emotional disorders discovered by screening and case-finding functions. Most of the projects (sixteen) are located in large state hospitals funded under the HIP Program. Their day hospital, day care treatment center, foster home programs, etc. have the facilities and staff to offer service once the need is discovered. Nursing and ward aides, case aides, and group work aides help provide children, adolescents, and adults with such alternatives to hospitalization as foster homes, home care, etc. A mental health center in an agency for children tries to prevent trauma for blind children by offering on-the-spot psychiatric first aid for those who appear emotionally upset. A few remaining projects with this goal pattern are located in community mental health clinics and social agencies.

GOAL PATTERN 5: TERTIARY PREVENTION

The vast majority of these projects (78 out of 108) give treatment in institutional care settings—hospitals, rehabilitation centers, halfway houses. Similar to the people helped in projects with previously described goal patterns, most of these patients are poor and socially deprived, needing considerable referral to welfare, housing, and other concrete services.

For this group of patients, burdened by mental as well as financial problems, the volunteers and paid nonprofessionals use their special skills and personality attributes to restore the patient's confidence in himself, and to find resources in the community to continue the process of resocialization and rehabilitation.

The twenty-six projects not located in institutional or clinic settings indicate that the relationship between inpatient and clinic settings with the tertiary level of prevention is not an exclusive one. Represented here are the patients and former patients who are maintained in the community through home care, foster homes, and a wide variety of social clubs and other innovative facilities for rehabilitation of former patients.

GOAL PATTERN 6: ALL LEVELS OF PREVENTION OR EXCEPTIONS TO THE CONTINUUM

Although it is the smallest (only twelve projects), this final group, which does not conform to the preventive continuum, is in many ways the most interesting. As one would expect, judging by the multiplicity of goals, the programs are highly ambitious. Probably strongly influenced by current concepts in the community mental health movement, these state hospitals, alcoholism and drug addict centers, and community mental health centers are committed to providing the entire range of preventive, educational, and therapeutic services for sick and well populations.

All share some emphasis on primary prevention. One state hospital project offers consultation to the local Head Start program, lectures for the community, outpatient clinic care, and special treatment programs for disturbed adolescents and geriatric patients. A community council provides opportunities for utilizing the talents of the aged to solve community-wide problems. The chronically ill aged are identified and offered appropriate services; the "normal" aged become occupied with important community tasks. One hospital homemaker program for the families of hospitalized patients has goals on two separate levels: (1) To provide parent-substitutes with the financial resources to keep together families threatened with disintegration because of a parent's hospitalization (primary prevention); and (2) to remain in the home after the patient's discharge from the hospital and offer supportive counseling based on the recommendations of the psychiatric and social work staff of the hosiptal (tertiary prevention).

The utilization of nonprofessionals is particularly interesting in these projects. The nonprofessionals offer substantial help in educating the community, and in case-finding, they locate the milder and more serious disorders in the community requiring aid. This is very much in contrast to their role in the projects which focus exclusively on secondary prevention (Goal Pattern 3). Here it is only the professionals who are given responsibility to implement the project goal of locating a problem group.

In this microcosm of projects, which includes both preventive and therapeutic goals, necessity apparently provides the stimulus for intervention. Projects with multiple, ambitious goals may be pressed to allow nonprofessionals to help with the process of spotting new or early cases of disorder (a process usually assumed to be the exclusive domain of the professional). The fact that they are allowed in these projects to work toward this goal is not in itself significant; that this goal seems to be singled out as the one toward which they have made their greatest contribution, however, is significant despite the small number of projects involved.

GOAL PATTERNS RANKED INTO HIGHER AND LOWER PREVENTIVE LEVELS

Having analyzed the various goal patterns, our objective now is to synthesize the goal patterns into the three major preventive levels. The principle behind this organization is that goal patterns can be grouped according to the highest single goal level stressed in each project. For example, the final goal pattern described (6) was combined with Goal Patterns 1 and 2, since all of them share considerable emphasis on primary prevention. The goal patterns gain new meaning when they are organized into the three major preventive levels. The advantage of this is that one can dispose of the overlapping frequencies, and a unique classification of each project into a goal pattern becomes possible.

It should be stressed that the use of the terms "high," "moderate," and "low" does not imply any invidious ranking of greater or lesser importance or value of primary, secondary, or tertiary prevention. As noted previously, a comprehensive community mental health program requires appropriate attention to all goal levels. With the necessity of treating and rehabilitating large numbers of chronic mentally ill patients, planning a "high" level primary preventive goal would be most inappropriate. The only pragmatic goal would be one which focuses on reducing the rate of residual defect resulting from the process of mental disorder so that the chronically ill patient population can reach its highest potential level of functioning in the community.

Table 7.3 shows the final organization of goal patterns into

Table 7.3. Organization of Goal Patterns into Preventive Goal Levels

Preventive Goal Levels	No. of Projects	Percent (out of 100%)	Based on Goal Pattern Groups
High (Primary)	43	23%	1, 2, 6
Moderate (Secondary)	34	18%	3, 4
Low (Tertiary)	108	59%	5
Total No. of Projects	185		

high, moderate, and low preventive levels for all 185 projects. If we classify projects by single "highest" goal reported, the distribution is essentially similar to the other ways of examining goals. The majority (59 percent) stress the tertiary level. Less than one-fourth of the projects emphasize the primary level, and still fewer give the secondary level as their highest planned goal.

The next section makes use of the above-ranked goal patterns to study relationships with selected project characteristics and ratios of utilization of nonprofessionals.

RELATIONSHIP OF PREDOMINANT GOAL, SELECTED PROJECT CHARACTERISTICS, AND USE OF NONPROFESSIONALS

As Table 7.4 indicates, there is a strong relationship between the type of setting and the preventive goal level. Obviously, certain settings lend themselves to certain goals, and vice versa.

136

Table 7.4. Projects With Goals at Each Preventive Level
by Project Setting[a]

| Project Setting | Preventive Goal Level (in percent) | | | |
	Primary	Secondary	Tertiary	
Institutional Care				
(104 projects)	7	18	75	(100%)
Mental Health Clinics and Social Agencies				
(24 projects)	29	42	29	(100%)
Community Setting				
(34 projects)	62	9	29	(100%)
Multiple Settings				
(23 projects)	35	9	56	(100%)
Total Number of Projects (185)				

[a] See Table 7.3 for number of projects at each goal level; 43 at primary level, 34 at secondary level, and 108 at tertiary level.

Institutional care settings tend to have tertiary preventive goals. On the other hand, community settings, such as schools, settlement houses, and public health facilities, lend themselves largely to primary preventive goals. It is not possible, however, to say that the child guidance clinics, community mental health clinics, and social agencies focus predominantly on the secondary preventive level. Thus, we cannot presume that these settings are geared chiefly to case finding, early location of emotional disorders, etc., even though for many of them this was the original intention. Nineteen out of thirty-four projects characterized as having secondary preventive goals were located in institutional settings (chiefly mental hospitals).

One can say definitively, however, that the expectation of finding increasing numbers of projects located in institutional settings as one moves from primary, through secondary to the tertiary levels respectively, is well borne out by the NIMH Study.

NONPROFESSIONAL FUNCTIONS AND GOAL LEVELS

There are indications that certain types of goals cluster with certain types of activities, all of which are geared to a specific level of prevention. This data will have more meaning when it is given in the context of the development of the index of prevention, the subject of the second section of this chapter. Suffice to say here that cross-tabulations yielded significant relationships between nonprofessional functions and project goal levels (refer to Table 7.5).

Table 7.5. Relationship Between Nonprofessional Functions and Project Goal Levels

Function	Level of Significance[a]
Casefinding and project goal level	(.02)
Caretaking function and project Goal level	(.05)
Group Counseling and Project Goal Level	(.001)
Activity Therapy and Project Goal Level	(.001)
Milieu Therapy and Project Goal Level	(.01)

[a] Regarding Chi Square Probability Level, it is to be noted that two-tailed tests were used on all data to provide a conservative estimate of significant relationship.

With the exception of the casefinding function, all of the above functions are proportionately more related to the tertiary level of prevention than would be expected by chance; that is, there is strong probability that one would find nonprofessionals performing functions to help rehabilitate the severely mentally ill.

GOALS AND RATIO OF USE OF NONPROFESSIONALS

Significance was found also in the relationship between project goal patterns and the ratio of paid nonprofessionals to professionals (.01 probability level).

The proportion of projects with high ratios of paid nonprofessionals to professionals is greater for tertiary goals than for primary or secondary goals. *This is contrary to the assumption that nonprofessionals would be more highly utilized in relation to promoting community mental health for the population-at-large than for the more clinical activities usually required in working with the mentally ill.*

The over-all picture is quite different for volunteers where there was no evidence of relationship between their use and project goals. One can only report the trend that all projects, regardless of goal orientation, tended to have low ratios of volunteers to professionals or none at all. Considering that the vast majority of projects utilizing volunteers reported that their services more than justified the expense of training and supervision, it would appear that volunteers are not being utilized fully enough in relation to mental health goals at any level of prevention.

The next section makes use of data derived from the study of goals in the development of an index of prevention.

PREVENTION AND INNOVATION IN THE STUDY PROJECTS

The preceding section described and analyzed planned project goals illustrative of primary, secondary, and tertiary prevention. The best laid plans to achieve one or another level of prevention can be undone by a multitude of factors. One cannot promote mental health for the community-at-large, for example, without developing certain types of services and special types of care consistent with the needs of the appropriate client populations. In an effort to begin to measure preventive efforts in the NIMH projects, and nonprofessional roles in these efforts, an index of prevention was developed.

PURPOSES OF INDEX

An important question underlying the index formation was: "Under what conditions can we say that a project is attempting to deal with critical issues in the prevention of mental illness?" The previous section indicated that most NIMH projects focus on long-term treatment of patients who are already severely disabled, a finding which raises further questions: Do such projects really have a role in prevention? Is the term "tertiary prevention" used to classify these projects a mere euphemism? Under what conditions can such projects engage in preventive roles?

Five variables based on conceptual grounds as well as on statistical study were selected as logically relevant indicators for a prevention index (refer to Appendix C for details). These indicators were weighed equally, and scores for each indicator were added together to form a project's preventive index score. The 185 project scores were then divided into three groups: high, medium, and low prevention index scores. Scores ranged from 4 to 15, divided into: low (4-6), medium (7-9), and high (10-15).

The five components of the index form a matrix which will be presented to show their statistical interrelationships. In addition, meaningful relationships between the prevention index scores, selected project characteristics, and ratios of use of nonprofessionals will be presented.

Many factors, other than planned goals were introduced into the prevention index so as to measure more comprehensively the totality of efforts at prevention. A disadvantage of this broader view is that each item selected could not receive the attention in depth which was given to planned project goals.

COMPONENTS OF THE INDEX

The following five variables were chosen as the major significant components of the index, and weighted equally: goal patterns; mental health status of project population (diagnosed, not diagnosed); age of project population; selected professional and nonprofessional activities; and type of care given by project (alternative to hospitalization).

The rationale for choosing some of the components of the index (for example, goal patterns and mental health status) has already been discussed. Other components, beginning with the age of project population, have not. Many writers on mental health have theorized that, other considerations being equal, *the earlier in the life span that one pays attention to signs of emotional disturbance, the better are chances of preventing serious mental breakdown during later periods of life.* Practitioners, before and since Freud, have observed that pathological patterns tend to be more difficult to change as the individual grows older. Accepting this logic, treatment of children was therefore rated high. Adolescents and adults were given medium and low ratings respectively.

For "selected professional and nonprofessional activities" there were many more considerations. The nature of the program, the amount of time spent by professionals in community services, certain nonprofessional activities, etc. were scored indi-

141

vidually and combined into one composite score. Specifically preventive programs such as "family life education" were scored higher than more general community planning and consultation efforts. Accepting the premise that prevention efforts must be increasingly directed to *whole* populations, credit was given to projects which held large community meetings. Certain non-professional functions performed for the community-at-large were also singled out as statistically and substantively significant (for example, case-finding, tutoring, and retraining). A few other activities, such as crisis intervention, reality counseling, community improvement, were not performed by sufficient numbers of persons to achieve statistical significance, but were nevertheless scored as substantively significant.

The final item in the index, type of care, relates basically to the question of *whether or not hospitalization could be prevented.* There is no need to document here the high cost of hospitalization of the mentally ill in human and economic terms. Organized clinic and community-care programs (home care, social agency rehabilitative care, etc.) obviously provide alternatives for individuals who might otherwise require total hospitalization. Highest scoring was therefore accorded to the community-care programs with forms of service delivery most unlike the hospital facility providing only inpatient care. Appendix C gives complete scoring for index items.

STATISTICAL INTERRELATIONSHIP OF INDEX ITEMS

As seen in Table 7.6, statistical interrelationships among all the variables in the index well exceed the statistical margin of chance. That is, there is significance in the numerous interrelationships among the goals of a project, the mental health of the

142

RESEARCH FINDINGS IN PREVENTION AND INNOVATION

project population, the age of the project population, and the
activities and the type of care given.[3]

Table 7.6. Interrelationships Among Preventive Index Components[a]

Goal Patterns	Mental Health of Proj. Population	Age of[b] Proj. Popul.	Selected Prof. & Nonprof. Activities	Type of Care
Goal Patterns	.001	.001	.001	.001
		.02		
Mental Health of Proj. Pop.		.001	.001	.001
		.01		
Age of Proj. Population			.05	.001
			.01	.01
			.50	.05
Selected Prof. & Nonprof. Activities				.001

[a] Figures represent Chi Square Probability Levels.

[b] For age of population, projects serving children, adolescents, and adults were cross-tabulated separately with all other items. As a result, more than one figure representing Chi Square Probability Level may have resulted. If two separate figures are given, the first represents children and adolescents; the second represents the cross-tabulation with the adult population. If three figures are given, they represent separate Chi Square Probability Level figures for children, adolescents, and adults, in that order.

[3] The only exception is found in the relationship between selected professional-nonprofessional activities, and the adult project population. Nevertheless, there is a 10 percent differential in the direction of higher "selected activity" scores for projects serving children and adolescents compared with projects serving adults.

143

Of the ten major interrelationships on which the matrix is based, a few of the most revealing findings will be presented. Thus, projects dealing with nondiagnosed populations are significantly more likely to formulate more preventively-oriented goals, to serve younger age-groups, to carry on specifically preventive programs (for example family life education), and to concentrate on the less traditional nonhospital types of care.

Similarly, projects serving children and adolescents are more likely to formulate preventive-oriented goals (see Table 7.7), to deal with nondiagnosed populations, and to carry on specifically preventive programs. All of the findings concerning age groups confirm our assumption that serious concern with prevention of mental illness demands that priority be given to earlier periods of the total life span. This does not mean that adult needs should be sacrificed. Considerably more efforts at the most basic preventive level need to be made on behalf of adults, who, after all, are the parents and caregivers of the young.

Table 7.7. Number of Projects which Serve Children, Adolescent, and Adult Clients by Preventive Goal Score

			Preventive Goal Score			
		Total				
Age Group of		No. in	Low	Moderate	High	
Clients[a]		age group	(%)	(%)	(%)	
Children	(High Score)	58	31	24	45	(100%)
Adolescents	(Mod. Score)	71	38	23	39	(100%)
Adults	(Low Score)	140	64	17	19	(100%)

[a] Based on 185 projects. Duplications result from the fact that many projects served more than one age group. Percents are based on a total of a given age group.

GENERAL FINDINGS OF THE PREVENTION INDEX

The previous section has presented the components within the prevention index and a matrix of its statistical interrelationships. The over-all findings of the prevention index will now be given.

Table 7.8. Distribution of Scores of Preventive Index

Score	Number of proj.	Percent
High	63	34
Medium	76	41
Low	46	25
Total	185 projects	100%

A new perspective on prevention efforts in NIMH projects emerges from this distribution of preventive index scores (refer to Table 7.8). Three-fourths of the projects score medium or high on the prevention index. Only one-fourth have low scores. This is quite different from the analysis of the goals, which showed that the majority of the projects had low planned preventive goal scores. *Why the difference?*

The number of projects treating the mentally ill in psychiatric hospitals is considerably higher than the number of projects with low preventive index scores. One-hundred-forty projects treat the mentally ill, whereas only forty-six are found in the "low" preventive score category. Obviously, many of those projects planning to treat only those who are already severely ill (low, tertiary preventive goal level) must be making substantial efforts to prevent their patients' continued illness or to prevent similar illness for others in the community. A considerable number of the projects serving the chronic and severely ill also offer treatment services to children and adolescents, profes-

145

sional consultation services to the community, and nonprofessional services which are considered to be relevant to prevention (for example, home finding and tutoring).

The remainder of the projects with high or moderate preventive index scores are, as one would expect, many of the same projects which stressed primary or secondary preventive goals, those which planned to promote community mental health, to reach the underprivileged, school dropouts, and others through appropriate preventive activities.

THE PREVENTIVE INDEX AND PROJECT CHARACTERISTICS

One purpose of developing the preventive index score was to see if there were any significant differences between project scores depending on where they are located, type of setting, and ratio of utilization of nonprofessionals.

SIZE OF CITY

The general relationship between preventive index scores and the size of population appears to exceed the statistical margin of chance. The largest (500,000 or over) and second largest

Table 7.9. Number of Projects with Type of Setting by Prevention Index Score

| Prevention Index Score | Type of Setting | | | |
	Institutional Care (N = 104) *Percent*	Mental Health Clinic & Social Agency (N = 24) *Percent*	Community Setting (N = 34) *Percent*	Multiple Setting (N = 23) *Percent*
Low	37	13	3	17
Medium	49	29	26	39
High	14	58	71	44
	100%	100%	100%	100%

146

(25,000 to 499,999) city categories have a higher proportion of high and medium preventive index scores, respectively, than do the smaller cities and towns (less than 25,000).

TYPE OF SETTING

As can be noted in Table 7.9, the findings are clear-cut for different types of settings. Seventy-one percent of the projects in community settings (for example, settlement houses, schools) have high preventive index scores, compared with fewer (58 percent) in mental health clinic settings, and very few (14 percent) in institutional care settings.

RATIO OF USE OF NONPROFESSIONALS AND PREVENTIVE INDEX SCORE

The general pattern of ratios of utilization of paid nonprofessionals in all projects follows logically from the above findings. The highest percentage of projects with high preventive index scores (49 percent) have relatively low ratios of paid nonprofessionals to professionals. These tend to be located largely in the community settings which, as we discussed above, tend to employ fewer paid nonprofessionals than the institutional care settings. One possible explanation is that the community settings are just beginning to use nonprofessionals, in contrast to institutional care settings which have always depended on nonprofessionals for supportive and maintenance services. As noted previously, the volunteer ratio is not statistically significant in comparison with the preventive index score because of the general pattern of low ratio of use of volunteers for most projects.

INNOVATION IN INDIVIDUAL PROJECTS

To what extent do individual projects make "innovative" use of nonprofessional community mental health personnel? If the utilization of nonprofessionals is occurring for the first time in the history of the sponsoring agency, we consider this "innovative." Clearly, this does not mean that these activities are necessarily innovative for the entire field of mental health throughout the country. For example, establishing a community mental health clinic in one isolated rural area may constitute an "innovation" for that area, but it is hardly an innovative activity for many other locales in this nation.

"Innovation" (first time use) is measured along several dimensions. We were interested not only in the basic questions of whether the sponsoring agency was using nonprofessionals for the first time, but also in the following questions: Is the project attempting to reach groups which the sponsoring agency had not previously served? What types of care are being given which were not previously provided by the sponsoring agency? Is the project attempting to have nonprofessionals perform functions not previously given? Is the project trying to recruit and train persons not previously considered eligible for careers in the human services field?

A total of twelve such questions formed the innovative index. A simple, additive score was devised. Each "innovative" item was scored one point, with the exception of the basic item regarding utilization of nonprofessionals for the first time in the sponsoring agency (this received two points). The score value for each project ranged, therefore, from zero to a maximum

Table 7.10. Distribution of Innovative Index Scores

Innovative Score	Number of Projects (out of 185)	Percent of Projects (out of 100%)
High	60	32.5
Moderate	75	40.5
Low	50	27.0

score of thirteen. The projects were then divided into three groups: high, moderate, or low on innovation.[4]

The distribution of scores is shown in Table 7.10. As can be seen, nearly three-fourths of the projects scored moderately or highly innovative according to our criteria for "innovation." Having nonprofessionals perform functions which sponsoring agencies had not previously provided proved to be the single, most frequently mentioned "innovative" response (109 projects). Other oft-mentioned responses included reaching out to client groups not previously served (82 projects); offering new types of care (73 projects); and attempting to recruit or train nonprofessionals for new service functions (97 and 90 projects, respectively).

Similar items in both the innovative and preventive indices tended to produce scores in the same direction. Thus, the apparent relationship between the two indices is not of substantive significance because of some overlapping of items. For example, it should be noted that the "newer" types of care, for example, home care, would tend to score both "innovative" and "preventive."

Possibly because of the way in which innovation is defined, there is little influence of the type and location of setting on the innovative index. No one particular size of city or location scored significantly higher in the innovative index than another.

---

[4] Scores of 5 to 13 were rated high; 3 to 4 were rated moderate; and 0 to 2 were low.

8

EVALUATION OF NONPROFESSIONALS

RATIONALE FOR NONPROFESSIONALS

Reasons for using nonprofessionals could be described broadly either as an expedient response to the professional manpower shortage or a response to different conceptions of service (increased emphasis on bridging, expediting, and personal socializing relationships provided by nonprofessionals).

Most of the 1968 NIMH Study projects reported multiple bases for use of nonprofessionals. The vast majority reported the combination of special attributes of the nonprofessionals, the need to extend service programs, and the professional manpower shortage as reasons for their use of nonprofessionals.

The personal attributes of nonprofessionals most often sought were flexibility, spontaneity, enthusiasm, and commitment. The most frequently mentioned single reason for using nonprofessionals was the need to "provide informal sustaining relationships to patients and clients" (70 percent of the projects). This suggests that many believe that as society becomes more impersonal, urbanized, and automated, the need increases for personal and socializing relationships which the nonprofessional person is able to provide.

The next most frequently mentioned reason was the need to relieve the professional of tasks not requiring professional expertise (66 percent of the projects). Almost 60 percent used nonprofessionals because they felt they could communicate better with the patient-client groups or reduce the oft-cited problems of "social distance" between professional and patient group.

Comparatively fewer (40 percent) reported the use of nonprofessionals to provide services which would be better provided by professional staff if enough were available (most expedient reason). One-half of the projects were concerned with training for new service functions and about one-third with recruiting and training of persons not previously considered eligible for careers in the human services field.

Although mentioned least among the major reasons for utilization of nonprofessionals, a significant percentage of the projects (57 percent) were concerned with stimulating volunteer activity, either for the purpose of increasing general citizen participation in community service programs or improving community understanding of mental health programs.

Without going into the issue of whether professionals can or should do certain jobs, the consensus is that there are certain human needs for understanding, warmth, friendship, and concrete problem-solving which nonprofessionals are considered capable of providing for the mentally ill and for others in the community. Nonprofessional roles, based on fulfilling these needs, serve dual functions: (1) The services given to the mentally ill and to the total community are extended and enriched by use of the special capabilities and roles of the nonprofessional; and (2) the mental health professional is freed to utilize his specific expertise in therapy and/or other functions.

Statistically less significant, but nevertheless meaningful, are several other reasons given for use of nonprofessional personnel. Among such reasons is the development of paid, indigenous leadership in ghetto communities to serve as a model

151

for self-help and institutional change for the entire community.

We often find that poor, "indigenous" nonprofessionals do serve as more successful social learning models for their deprived, undereducated neighbors than middle-class or professional persons. Efforts to introduce family planning in one neighborhood were totally unsuccessful until an outreach program, using only women indigenous to the neighborhood, was initiated. The paid professional staff, women of Puerto Rican background, were satisfied users of birth control methods, recently taught to them by the family planning clinic staff; they ventured forth to visit the homes of their friends and neighbors in a low-income area, communicated their own satisfaction with family planning education, and related to the questions and concerns of their clients. This informal, social, educational model changed the neighborhood family planning program from an almost defunct operation to a model of successful service-delivery in a short span of time.

Theoretical confirmation for greater success in the use of "indigenous" persons to educate their peers has been found earlier in the work of Kurt Lewin. Experimental efforts to teach mothers to improve the diet of their children (for example, through greater milk consumption) became successful only when one peer-group accepted this change in child-rearing, and became natural leaders in the drive to convert their neighbors to better nutritional habits.[1] The theory, tested by Lewin, that people learn more readily from their peer-group than other groups, is apparently receiving substantial confirmation from current experiments in the use of indigenous personnel.

---

[1] Kurt Lewin, "Forces behind food habits and methods of change." Bulletin of the National Research Council, 1943, p. 108.

ASSESSMENT OF CONTRIBUTION

The project directors in the 1968 NIMH Study were asked to assess the contribution of nonprofessional staff to the functioning of their projects. Responses were analyzed along the following dimensions: (1) Contribution of nonprofessional staff to project goal achievement; (2) nonprofessional contribution to improvements in service to project population; (3) interaction with professional staff (positive and negative elements); (4) career outcomes for nonprofessionals, and terminated projects outcomes; and (5) suggested changes in future utilization of nonprofessionals based on problems and obstacles revealed.

In addition, opinions were elicited about the over-all justification of the use of nonprofessionals in terms of expenses of training and supervision. The question of whether the nonprofessional staff would still be utilized if sufficient professional staff and funds were available was considered basic to the assessment.

It should be noted that respondents faced a difficult and complex task in assessing their use of nonprofessionals. Myriad economic and human cost factors were involved. Essentially, most of the projects were experimenting with new service programs. Utilization of nonprofessionals was an instrument toward changing goals of care to project populations. Introducing changes of several types, and on many levels, simultaneously compounded the problems of assessment.

In addition, there were some practical limitations. Respondents for current projects, especially those which were in operation for a year or less than a year, indicated that it was too early to assess such factors as nonprofessional contribution to goal achievement. (Fortunately, very few projects were in operation for such a short period of time.) On the other hand, project directors of terminated projects were faced with the opposite problems; namely, too much time might have elapsed for accurate recall. (Here, too, it was fortunate that the number of projects affected was quite small.) Also, the evaluative questions were frankly posed, and it would be naive to expect total objectivity in response to such questions.

GENERAL FINDINGS

Overwhelmingly, the project directors felt that the service performed by nonprofessionals justified the expense of training, supervision, and general agency overhead. This applied to both paid and volunteer staff (150 and 89 projects respectively). Nonprofessionals were viewed as having a "unique" role (152 projects) rather than an "expedient" role (28 projects). Since definitions of "unique" and "expedient" were not given, this finding cannot be taken too literally. By and large, nonprofessionals were not utilized in an attempt to fill the shoes of nonexistent professionals. There were two major patterns of use.

NEW ROLES

Appropriate new roles were created for nonprofessionals based on unmet client needs. It was felt that nonprofessionals could appropriately fill these new roles because of their special characteristics and the availability of training and supervision required to augment their natural abilities. The special "reachout" aide who brought a client into a family life education program and the psychiatric ward aide who followed a patient's progress in home treatment illustrate this pattern.

154

TRANSFERRED ROLES

Specific tasks previously performed by professionals were allocated and tailored to the nonprofessional's abilities within a total context which often became "unique" to the nonprofessional. An example would be the assignment of an activity therapy or milieu therapy role to a nonprofessional psychiatric technician or occupational therapy aide. The need for the patient to have a positive ego-strengthening relationship with one staff member within a hospital may be of paramount consideration rather than the therapeutic skill or lack of skill of the aide. The specific way in which the role is performed may be tailored to the particular capabilities and background of the nonprofessional.

Regardless of the pattern of use, the overwhelming consensus of opinion was that "nonprofessionals have an important contribution to make." The following comment was typical: "I believe every effort should be made to utilize appropriate selected nonprofessional personnel in comprehensive mental health programs, if an equal effort is made to provide the necessary training and supervision."

UTILIZATION PREFERENCES

The question of whether, given the choice of hiring professionals, project directors would prefer to utilize nonprofessionals for those functions which professionals previously performed, received responses displayed in Table 8.1.

A few respondents wrote that both staffs are equally valuable or that they did not know what they would do if they could choose nonprofessionals for tasks performed previously by professionals. These responses are open to considerable interpretation. The largest single number (55) state that they clearly

Table 8.1. Utilization Preference

Utilization Preference	No. of Projects Responding
Would clearly utilize professional staff	17
Would probably utilize professional staff	33
Uncertain	29
Would probably not utilize professional staff	36
Would clearly not utilize professional staff	55

would not utilize professional staff, which would appear to confirm previous findings that the nonprofessional is making a special contribution to mental health. These 55 projects were analyzed separately to see if any significant patterns existed. One very interesting finding came to light. More than three-fourths of these 55 projects were Mental Health projects which function in more diversified mental health agency settings in contrast to hospital settings. (This distribution differs significantly from that of MH versus HIP projects in our over-all study sample.)[2]

This large majority of MH projects tended to use more of the innovative type staff, such as tutors, home visitors, special skill and reach-out aides, rather than the more traditional personnel. Paid and volunteer staff were reported as being well represented. In some staff categories such as home visitor and "other" titles, volunteer categories were reported by proportionately more projects than paid categories.

In contrast, analysis of the 17 projects at the other end of the scale (that is, projects that would clearly prefer to utilize

---

[2] Out of the 185 projects, 61 percent are MH against 39 percent which are HIP, whereas 78 percent of this subsample of projects which prefer to continue using nonprofessionals are MH and only 22 percent are HIP projects.

professional staff) presents an entirely different picture. They are chiefly HIP (14 out of 17 projects) in the more conventional state hospital settings. They use far more traditional staff types, for example, nursing and ward aides, and occupational and physical therapy aides.

These findings lead to an understanding of the contributions of various nonprofessional staff in all mental health settings. They suggest that the services of nonprofessionals are clearly preferred over those of professionals in a number of tasks, particularly of volunteers and those with innovative titles.

A majority of projects, then, express direct conviction on the value of nonprofessionals. However, even those projects which express general preference for professional staff reveal that they value the special contribution of nonprofessionals in releasing professional time for therapeutic tasks requiring their expertise; there is, in other words, an indirect expression of the value of nonprofessional staff even among those projects which have a general preference for nonprofessionals.

CONTRIBUTION OF NONPROFESSIONALS
TO GOAL ACHIEVEMENT

Project goals in the 1968 NIMH Study represented a continuum from primary through secondary and tertiary prevention (refer to Chapter 7). On all the goals listed, there was a consistent pattern of greater numbers of responses indicating that nonprofessionals had contributed substantially or moderately rather than "little or none." In the treatment of the severely ill (tertiary prevention goal), there was a disproportionately higher number of responses indicating "substantial" contribution of nonprofessionals (70 percent) than is true for the other goals (ranging

157

from 33 to 45 percent).[3] Only for one goal—the case-location, secondary prevention goal—is the "moderate" contribution response slightly larger than the "substantial" response (37 percent "moderate," 33 percent "substantial" for 75 responses).

One would not expect that nonprofessionals could contribute substantially in so many projects to the treatment and rehabilitation of seriously disturbed persons. Nonprofessionals would be expected to contribute heavily in programs geared for the most part to planning and providing for general community mental health (equated with primary prevention). As anticipated, contributions to primary prevention and citizen participation goals were found for nonprofessionals.

But it does not follow that the nonprofessional's role in secondary prevention should be rejected. Nonprofessional opportunities on this preventive level have not been sufficiently tested experimentally. Possibly, when projects are motivated to allow nonprofessionals to carry out certain functions, and to offer them sufficient guidance and supervision to engage in such tasks as clinical case finding, the nonprofessional may become able to make a greater contribution to early location of suspected mental illness.

CONTRIBUTION TO IMPROVEMENTS IN SERVICE TO PROJECT POPULATION

Table 8.2 lists selected improvements in project service, with data on the number of projects reporting substantial, moderate, slight, or no nonprofessional contribution to each service.

---

[3] The over-all distribution of degree of goal achievement is different for the tertiary prevention goal, too. Fifty-five projects reported that their goal of providing for treatment and rehabilitation of the mentally ill was "fully achieved."

As seen in Table 8.2, whenever an improvement in service actually occurred, the nonprofessional's contribution to the service improvement was most often rated as "substantial." Nonprofessionals helped projects substantially in servicing more

Table 8.2. Contributions by Nonprofessionals to Improvements in Service

(Given in percent of total no. of responses)

Improvements in service	Projects reporting degree of nonprofessional contribution			
	Substantial	Moderate	Slightly or not at all	Total No. of project responses
Service initiated and completed faster	54	31	15	80
Able to serve more people	59	32	9	127
New services provided	57	27	16	141
More professional time made available for treatment	45	31	24	106
New viewpoints gained by project staff re: population served	53	31	16	135

people, offering new services, and providing the project staff with new viewpoints in regard to the project population.

For homemaking and liaison roles, nonprofessionals were indispensable. One project director reported: "We are completely sold on these homemakers; we only wish we could afford more of them." Another project director commented that "it was with pleasure that we recognized that our use of lay volunteers as links to the community resulted in a real benefit not only to this organization but many other organizations in the county." And another reported that "the use of volunteers has enhanced

159

the image of public welfare and given the community some insight into the services provided as well as showing the financial responsibility of a county welfare department."

A credit union, whose reasonable rates now protect community residents from the exploitation of local loan sharks, could never have been achieved without the zeal of hard-working, indigenous nonprofessional residents of an urban ghetto area. This same group, working with their local priest, recently concentrated their energies on planning to construct a low-cost housing development in their deteriorating neighborhood.

Some "other improvements in service" included qualitative changes: a change of atmosphere within the agency, and more lively and vital relationships among staff or between patients and staff. A project seeking to facilitate the return of patients from hospital to the community felt that the use of nonprofessionals provided a more relaxed, informal "nontreatment" approach, which was exactly what was needed by patients and the outside community. Improved morale, better attitudes toward patients, definite improvement in over-all quality of service, were other improvements reported. The addition of youthful, untrained personnel within several hospitals made the older trained personnel re-examine their own roles and the role, structure, and function of the entire hospital.

In the bulk of the institutional care settings, nonprofessionals (chiefly psychiatric nursing aides, case aides, and other therapeutic aides) are making an important contribution to improved patient service by freeing professionals for treatment activity which they should properly perform. As indicated before, this is not to imply that project directors would not prefer to utilize professionals for many of the therapeutic tasks now being performed by their nonprofessional staff if sufficient professional staff became available. However, given the reality of acute professional manpower shortages, necessity has provided the opportunity for teaching nonprofessionals certain therapeutic tasks which they might never have been allowed to learn. It also suggests that nonprofessionals possess special capabilities which could be developed in order to free the professional of the future for essential professional tasks.

INTERACTION BETWEEN PROFESSIONALS AND NONPROFESSIONALS

Table 8.3 lists the interaction experiences (both positive and negative) between professionals and nonprofessionals. A frequency distribution of the number of projects which reported

Table 8.3. Interaction Between Professional and
Nonprofessional Staff

Interaction experiences	Projects utilizing paid staff	Projects utilizing volunteer staff
Provides experience in supervision for professional staff	84	17
Overlapping of functions between professionals and nonprofessionals	60	5
Expanded professional staff's understanding of client-group through association with nonprofessionals	69	15
Required additional professional time for training and supervision	67	14
Caused communication problems	33	5
Status competition between the two groups	34	2

161

particular advantages or disadvantages is also supplied in relation to their paid and volunteer staff.

As may be noted, the four most frequently reported interaction experiences applicable to paid nonprofessional staff contained both positive and negative features. On the plus side, collaboration between professionals and nonprofessionals provided experience in supervision for professional staff, and expanded professional staff's understanding of client groups through association with nonprofessionals. Less advantageous were the additional professional time required for training and supervision and the overlapping of functions between professionals and nonprofessionals. Communication problems and status competition between professionals and nonprofessionals were reported as affecting relatively small numbers of projects for both paid and volunteer workers.

Illustrative of other interaction problems was the difficulty in simultaneously training nonprofessionals of vastly differing educational backgrounds; that is, the less-educated rehabilitation aides began to feel resentful of the more knowledgeable college-educated aides who showed themselves in a more favorable light in the learning situation. Overlapping of roles among professionals themselves was seen, too, as a potential source of conflict which seeps through from the professional to the nonprofessional level.

In one project, conflict arose out of overlapping roles between physicians and nurses. Until this professional team conflict was resolved in a hospital ward, the nonprofessional attendants and nursing aides became uncertain about their roles. However, as the team conflict was resolved, the entire team of professionals and nonprofessionals began to function more constructively and with markedly less evidence of status competition.

162

Not always, however, were friction and competition resolved positively. In another project, in which nonprofessionals were given substantial community organization responsibility in a highly innovative social action endeavor, some nonprofessionals began to express the belief, after a short period of performance, that they could handle the professional social worker's job and should therefore receive equal status and salary. It was noted that when professionals and nonprofessionals demonstrate their respective insecurity by depreciating each other the effectiveness of both is diminished. In general, it was noted that there was less likelihood of status competition when professionals were more secure and competent in their professional roles.

INTERACTION EXPERIENCES BY STAFF CATEGORY

Traditional nonprofessional staff (case aides, nursing aides, recreation aides, etc.) tended to be much more involved in all interaction experiences. One explanation may be that the traditional nonprofessional tends to work in a more structured institutional setting where he comes into close and frequent contact with many professional core disciplines. On the other hand, the innovative nonprofessional generally functions more independently of the professional in the community at large.

It would appear that the differing role expectations between traditional and innovative staff groups were related to communication and status problems. Although tutors often performed many functions other than tutoring, they were still expected primarily to excel in tutoring. Music or dance therapists were expected to have special expertise in music or dance even though they may have engaged in milieu, activity, and other therapeutic tasks.

Having one's own area of expertise, apart from the usual

163

team tasks performed jointly by professionals and nonprofessionals, apparently puts the nonprofessional into less competition with the professional. His contribution can be made without his becoming as closely involved in all ways with his professional colleagues. Significantly, the only innovative staff which had communication and status problems similar to those of the traditional staff were the community mental health aides. It will be recalled that these aides were expected to perform the same wide range of functions usually assignd to the traditional case and nursing aides. No one task was considered to belong to them uniquely. Typically, they worked in the hospitals and were involved in the hierarchical structure of professional teams.

ATTEMPTS TO REDUCE INTERACTION PROBLEMS

The use of both individual and group conferences was mentioned frequently as a means of airing grievances and learning to communicate. Some projects had daily meetings in hopes of solving problems before a crisis arose. Others set aside a portion of time at the end of each workday to ventilate reactions to experiences that had occurred during the day. This was particularly successful for those staff working with highly disturbed individuals, especially children with psychotic or behavior disorders.

One project had a two-week planning workshop prior to the beginning of the project operation, which was attended by all staff. This gave nonprofessionals the chance to participate in the planning of the program in addition to having informal contacts with professionals. Another project had both groups attend seminars and lectures together. This technique of simultaneous education offered nonprofessionals considerable status. Other projects found that a high quality of instruction and supervision

164

successfully reduced interaction problems. One project even planned to purchase additional psychiatric time for teaching. Others felt that by giving nonprofessionals additional responsibility they could enjoy smoother operations. One project allowed its nursing and ward aides to function with relative autonomy since they were the ones carrying the major responsibility for the project's total operation. Another allowed its nonprofessionals to participate in decisionmaking, and thus facilitate a greater sense of esteem and involvement. Any nonprofessional group which perceived that it was being neglected or left out of the team would tend to develop resentment.

A clear division of functions with every person knowing exactly what is expected of him is proposed by some respondents as a way of lessening confusion and conflict. One respondent noted, for example, that the project "placed their volunteer recreation and group work aides in groups where functions were more concrete and less complex, and explicit tasks were assigned by professionals in charge." In contrast, other respondents noted that "a sharp distinction is not functionally useful" and that a "redefinition of all roles is in order."

A factor held to be of paramount importance in the mental health of the professional and nonprofessional staff was the attitude of the project administration. The support and dedication of the institutional administration was essential for peaceful interaction of staff and constructive flow of energies.

TERMINATED PROJECT AND CAREER OUTCOMES

What happened to the projects upon termination? Did they become integrated into the continuing sponsoring agencies, and what other impact did they have on related community mental health agencies?

165

Use of the term "career outcomes" implies that the nonprofessional is working not merely on a job without a future but rather a job which could be designed as a rung on a mental health career ladder. Certain terms used in nonprofessional titles signal the status of the job as an entry onto a career ladder. Among these terms are "aide," "assistant," "apprentice," and "trainee." In the design of careers, particularly "new careers," titles are extremely important. They are "symbolic of the employer's commitment to the career concept and of the worker's choice of a career rather than a job."[4] Especially when the original title carries a low-status noncareer connotation (as is true of the ward aide or attendant title), employers and workers have been motivated to devise entirely new titles to suggest that the jobs are more than meet the eye and are actually career situations.

Although much is being written on the subject of the need for career lines, the actual implementation of this concept to date is unknown. One purpose of the 1968 NIMH Study was to determine what happened to the nonprofessional after leaving a terminated project. First, did he remain in the mental health field?

Almost half of the terminated projects (31) became part of on-going programs of their sponsoring agency. One-fifth of the projects became part of the on-going program of another agency in the community, such as the Department of Public Welfare, the Board of Health, the State Department of Mental Health, "Head Start" programs, and public schools.[5]

---

[4] Sidney A. Fine, *Guidelines for the Design of New Careers,* W. E. Upjohn Institute for Employment Research, Washington, D.C., 1967, p. 4.

[5] As indicated previously, all but 7 of the terminated 65 projects were the more diversified MH project programs rather than the HIP programs, which were characteristically situated in state hospital settings.

In a few cases, the entire sponsoring agency program was revamped as a result of the project's experiences. There are instances in which a State Parole Division and community narcotic rehabilitation programs have adopted *in toto* innovative programs, including the employment of large numbers of the indigenous nonprofessionals trained in these projects. Several of the ex-addicts have become articulate speakers, sought after by community groups.

In addition to rehabilitating themselves, the former addicts have learned how to help organize a daily regime calculated to work psychologically, intellectually, and socially to discourage a return to drug use. The ex-offenders are utilizing their recently learned counseling skills to communicate with current offenders and forestall recidivism. Paid employment and a regular work-schedule are, of course, excellent indicators of the success of the concept of self-help for individual offenders and addicts trained in projects geared to the treatment and rehabilitation of offenders and addicts.

The community is increasingly acknowledging the value of acquiring the kind of intimate knowledge of drug addiction, juvenile delinquency, alcoholism, etc. which former addicts, delinquents, and alcoholics possess. When a halfway house project for rehabilitating ex-addicts becomes a permanent part of the community in which it was originally located, the ideas of the project remain alive despite the project's formal termination.

The same can be said for a massive ghetto-located Neighborhood Service Center, which is an outgrowth of the experimental store-front center and funded by NIMH. The delivery of community preventive and therapeutic services, and particularly the large-scale use of indigenous nonprofessionals to deal with the mental health problems of the poor, remains a crucial feature of this neighborhood center as well as others currently being planned throughout the country and based on the model of terminated as well as current projects in this survey.

CAREER OUTCOMES

Almost two-thirds of the terminated NIMH projects report that their paid nonprofessionals are active in the mental health field. Either they now work in the sponsoring agency in the same or different capacity or they are working at another community agency in the mental health field. Several projects initiated training programs for mental health workers following project termination and set up different job descriptions for nonprofessional staff.

In one case, a plan evolved for graduates of the training programs to become members of the agency psychology department. These were college students trained as child therapists. In another project, volunteer interviewers became paid staff members. New nonprofessional staff categories were added in sponsoring agencies or related agencies. For example, in one community the teacher-aide job, introduced by the NIMH project, was adopted in the school system.

An outstanding leader in lay activities in the mental health field developed out of one project's experiences with volunteer case aides. Many of the volunteer case aides have continued to engage in volunteer activities in other areas within the sponsoring agency; several continued to visit patients in their homes long after the patients had been discharged from the state hospital. One volunteer case aide organized a local mental health association, and currently assumes a leadership role in planning and implementing the area's mental health program.

Practical nurses, trained in a state hospital project, have not only continued to work in the field but have also derived so much satisfaction from the opportunity to return to productive employment following marriage that they are continuing to recruit their women friends who want the opportunity for training to become nurses to the mentally ill.

A neighborhood improvement project, fighting deterioration of a community, has succeeded in turning apathetic citizens into community volunteer careerists bent on fighting for such matters of community concern as rezoning, street lighting, and helping of school dropouts.

One terminated project, featuring socioenvironmental therapy for chronic mental patients, reports that their training program is already paying substantial dividends: 15 out of the first 24 trainees are now employed at the hospital to provide the newer social interaction therapy on wards heretofore exclusively oriented toward custodial care. Of the nine remaining trainees, four are employed at a neighboring state hospital, one is employed by a private agency, providing services to chronic mental patients in the community, and two returned to graduate school following completion of training in the project.

Follow-up reports of teen-age youths trained as aides for child-care and mental health centers in a large city reveal strikingly good career outcomes for these youths, all of whom were high school dropouts, and several of whom had delinquent records.[6] Since termination of the training and demonstration project, all have been working as counseling aides in child care and mental health centers, city recreation programs, elementary schools, or welfare department institutions for dependent and delinquent children. A significant number of these aides have returned to school; at work their supervisors find them valuable

---

[6] William L. Klein. "The Training of Human Service Aides," in *Emergent Approaches to Mental Health,* New York: Appleton-Century-Crofts, pp. 158-61.

additions to program staff—eager to work, sensitive, often resourceful and innovative in carrying out their duties.

Possibly the best illustration of career outcomes of these disadvantaged youths is reflected in this observation of a seventeen-year-old tenth grade dropout who has been working for almost two years in a child care center.

The grammar is not the best, but the meaning is clear; In Day Care, I have learned many ways of handling kids. I also have learned how to cope with kids with home problems, shy, the ones that don't talk very much, the ones that get along with the rest of the group, how to play or what to play with on a rainy day. . . . it is alright to play with the kids but you must let them know that you are the teacher. . . . If I told you the way that I came up you won't believe it, but ever since I got this job I have learned and enjoyed every day of it.[7]

All of the above individual and project outcomes can be interpreted as signs of constructive change. Obviously, either the sponsoring agency or related community agencies deemed it beneficial to continue the project program and to utilize its concepts in some form, along with integration of the services of the project nonprofessionals with their own staff.

Fifteen percent of the projects reported that their nonprofessionals became employed in a different field of work, and about one-fifth of the terminated projects did not know what had become of their nonprofessionals after the project ended. Certainly, more rigorous follow-up of nonprofessionals (both paid and volunteer) would be meaningful in terms of planning their future utilization.

---

[7] Fishman et al., *New Careers* . . . , pp. 59-60.

SUGGESTED CHANGES IN UTILIZATION
OF NONPROFESSIONALS

A most important aspect of the NIMH Study was the suggestions of changes regarding all phases of utilization of nonprofessionals, from training, supervision, task assignment, to the final follow-up planning for them after their jobs had terminated.

RECRUITMENT, TRAINING AND SUPERVISION

A substantial number of respondents (71) indicated that changes did need to be made in the selection, training, and supervision of nonprofessionals. A common response was that more training was needed. This was often specified by suggestions for a planned, continuous process of training and supervision, stressing greater energy input in training at the very beginning of the process. It was suggested that training and supervision should be conceived and planned as an entity rather than separate unrelated units.

Many project directors perceived that the attitude of the trainer was the single most important factor in the success of the training program. The trainer must have a positive attitude toward the nonprofessionals both as individuals and as a group. When professionals held a deprecating attitude toward their nonprofessional colleagues and failed to acknowledge their positive attributes, the training and supervisory program was doomed to failure. This is not to suggest a romanticized attitude toward the nonprofessional.

The need for more careful selection was pointed out. It was found, for example, that some former mental patients were too closely identified with the patient group to make an objective contribution. College students, too, were sometimes prevented from establishing sustained relationships due to vaca-

171

tions, exams, etc. Neighborhood "indigenous" workers revealed, in some projects, serious authority problems and unrealistic competitiveness with professionals. Concrete suggestions, such as greater flexibility in recruiting part-time workers in hospitals, were also made.

TASK ASSIGNMENTS

That 122 project directors initially reasoned that they could utilize nonprofessionals to free professionals of tasks not requiring professional expertise offered a clue to the possibilities for change in task assignment, starting from the point of view of the professional and the professional task. A few, however, recommended less partialized task assignment as preferable. It was suggested, for example, that nursing aides be responsible for the total care of a limited number of patients so that the patients could benefit from this highly personal interest. Another project concerned with practical nurses suggested that much more responsibility could be given to their staff in observing selected patients over time, reporting their problem behavior, and participating in therapeutic care programs.

PERSONNEL ORGANIZATION

Thirteen of the terminated projects reported changes in the tables of personnel organization of the sponsoring agency as a result of utilization of nonprofessionals. A few projects (9) indicated that it would be impossible to hire nonprofessionals for their projects because of Civil Service restrictions. Fifty-five projects indicated that there would be delays or difficulties in the administrative personnel system governing their sponsoring agencies which would interfere with hiring successfully trained nonprofessionals from their projects.

172

These difficulties exist in all types of project settings, although the state hospital settings report proportionately greater difficulties. This group has been active in recommending loosening of Civil Service restrictions. For example, in New York State the Civil Service Commission has recently extended its age scale so that youngsters of 16 years of age with a work permit can apply for a civil service position. At the other end of the scale, any person up to 70 years of age can now apply for civil service status. Hospitals in New York are adopting these liberalized age criteria for staff, providing they pass physical examinations and meet other basic criteria.

REDUCING DISTINCTIONS BETWEEN PROFESSIONALS AND NONPROFESSIONALS

Some projects made a concerted effort at the outset to blur the distinctions between professionals and nonprofessionals; others found that, quite to their surprise, the distinctions disappeared of their own accord during the course of the project's life. Still others resisted labeling their staff as "nonprofessional," although they may have fit into the definition supplied in the Survey Instructions Manual.

For example, a trainer of teachers of mental health education wrote: "In our work we regard the nonprofessionals as professionals who are often superior to the usual professionals. What we have really done is developed a *new* professional group." Here, the experience and training of the nonprofessional provide him with skills and abilities which transform his stature from that of nonprofessional to that of professional.

Similarly, another respondent replied: "The contributions made by nonprofessionals makes the professional-nonprofessional distinction irrelevant." Another project, concerned with

173

easing the transition for patients from hospital to community, provided a one-year formal training period for all psychiatric technicians. The respondent felt that considering the length and the quality of this training, the term "nonprofessional" is not a completely accurate definition of the status of their psychiatric technicians.

Thus, as newer and improved training programs are initiated, distinctions between these two groups tend to become less relevant and, occasionally, disappear altogether. It should be noted, however, that the above comments apply to a small number of the reporting projects.

SUMMARY

The overwhelming majority of project directors reported that the advantages of using paid and volunteer nonprofessional staff greatly overshadowed the disadvantages. Strong recommendations were made for their future utilization in mental health.

Nonprofessionals were viewed as contributing to mental health in two unique ways: (1) filling new roles based on patient needs which were previously unfulfilled by any staff; and (2) performing parts of tasks previously performed by professionals, but tailoring the task to the nonprofessional's abilities. The result is that the task gestalt becomes "unique" to the nonprofessional.

The nonprofessional's contribution was most substantial toward the project goal of treating and rehabilitating the mentally ill (tertiary prevention). In hospital settings, nonprofessionals into an agency for the first time, or in new roles, does required professional expertise. The nonprofessional contributed fresh viewpoints in the course of providing "new services" to more people in need.

174

There were indications that the introduction of nonprofessionals into an agency for the first time, or in new roles, does affect the interpersonal and social systems of the project, both negatively and positively. New problems arise. Overlapping roles, communication and status strains, although not substantially reported, were significant considerations.

Generally, the introduction of nonprofessionals was perceived as infusing the projects with a new vitality, and forcing a self-evaluation which, although painful, led to beneficial changes for the field of mental health. Close to 90 percent of respondents surveyed indicated that their projects could not have functioned without utilization of the nonprofessional group.

9

IMPLICATIONS FOR THE SEVENTIES

RÉSUMÉ

To improve the nation's mental health, we must make better use of existing human resources. As the 1968 NIMH Project Study clearly shows, nonprofessionals are increasingly called on for a wide range of therapeutic and community improvement tasks. These activities have led to fresh ideas and new directions in alleviating manpower shortages in the mental health field.

The traditional boundary lines between the core mental health professional disciplines (psychiatry, social work, nursing, and psychology) are becoming blurred, and there is also a blurring of some traditional divisions between professional and nonprofessional functions. Inevitably, the dividing lines are becoming equally faint among the different nonprofessional aide groups which evolved in association with separate professional disciplines. Nonprofessional nursing aides, social work aides, vocational therapy aides, and psychiatric technicians are performing caretaking, therapeutic, and community-oriented functions with little apparent concern for such changes in their traditional roles. Tasks are being approached with a primary emphasis on the patient and his problems.

In the new mental health programs where goals are just beginning to be defined (for example, neighborhood service centers), a clear and firm definition of the nonprofessional's role could hardly be expected at this early stage of development.

In the older and more structured agency of the state mental hospital, the nonprofessional feels challenged to meet unfilled needs of patients which traditionally have been met by professionals. For example, nurses and psychiatric aides are learning to conduct group therapy because they perceive the value of such treatment for their patients. They know, too, that with the hospital's scarcity of customary psychiatrist and social worker group therapists, necessity demands a more functional approach to roles. To avoid taking on new tasks means patients' needs will remain unmet. The desire to answer the patients' cries for help, through appropriate therapies, appears to be superseding the fear of offending colleagues and of crossing previously guarded professional boundaries.

The 1968 NIMH Project Study produced evidence of a wide range of functions being performed by all nonprofessional staffs. The newer social relationship therapies for individuals and groups lead the list of most performed functions. And the nonprofessional has proven his ability to engage in human relationship roles with many different populations. Increasingly, he will be called on to deal with problems stemming from the social isolation and alienation endemic in our society.

An untrained person can develop both skill in observation of symptoms and ability to deliver personal care for the mentally ill. One study project reported that 80 percent of the nonprofessionals trained as practical nurses seemed capable of functioning in therapeutic roles (individual, group, and milieu therapy) in the care of the mentally ill. Where nonprofessionals worked with "normal" populations in the community, skills in community organization and in reducing the distance between the professional and the community were frequently noted. For innovative roles which nonprofessionals have been so often asked to assume—the teacher-mom, home-visitor, reach-out aide, etc.— the flexibility and spontaneity of nonprofessionals is seen as a primary asset. Generally, nonprofessionals are ready and willing to learn and to undertake more than is expected of them.

Although professionals and nonprofessionals work together on the same therapeutic and community tasks, certain functions tend to remain with the professional. Responsibility for the diagnostic and dynamic knowledge needed in screening and therapy still rests primarily with the professional. In addition, the mental health professional spends one-fifth of his time in teaching, training, and supervising nonprofessionals.

SUPERVISION AND TRAINING IMPLICATIONS

We are just beginning to understand some of the different implications of training and working with nonprofessionals. For those who have not graduated from high school, the old ways of recruiting and supervising nonprofessionals cannot be employed effectively without substantial changes. Program goals must be sufficiently clear to develop authentic pre-service training programs with a heavy component of on-the-job training methods, role-playing, and peer-group learning.

Since character and personality are considered to be more important per se than formal schooling in carrying out the newer social relationship roles, new informal screening methods must be developed, and methods of personality evaluation must be made more appropriate to the life-style of the typical applicant. Supervision which follows the clinical analytic model is often much too threatening to the "new" nonprofessional; group supervision helps dilute the critical impact of the often articulate professional trainer.

178

As the number of nonprofessionals increases, a new balance of power probably will emerge in relations between the two groups. Internal struggles for power and control based on color, ethnic identification, educational background, union affiliation, etc. can be anticipated in the course of a changing alliance between professionals and nonprofessionals, especially in crowded cities. Superiority of numbers may offer a ready forum to those nonprofessionals whose attitudes toward established authority are most hostile.

On the other hand, when the ratio of nonprofessional to professional is low, the Pygmalion tendency to mold the nonprofessional to the classical professional mold must be averted in the interests of developing the genuine potential of the nonprofessional. And the most knowledgeable professional cannot train the nonprofessional unless he comes to his task with a positive attitude and an open-minded willingness to learn from his new colleague. This presupposes, too, the scientist's aversion to promises and slogans of nonprofessional power which can only boomerang in the real world of self-interests.

FUNCTIONAL GROUPS

Nonprofessionals will work increasingly in agencies characterized by interdependence of varied auspices: national, state, and local; governmental, private, and nonprofit.

Traditional relationships between the structure and the function of agencies also are breaking down. It is not unusual for settlement houses and educational institutions to offer therapeutic programs. Certainly, the isolation of the mental hospital is decreased when state hospitals offer community mental health programs, homemaker services, and consultation to schools.

The typical recipient of mental health services is a poor,

mentally ill adult, black or white, with less than high school education. Pre- or post-hospital care at a state hospital, day hospital, or halfway house is generally given. Major emphases are on personal counseling, habit retraining, social rehabilitation, sheltered workshop, and job and home-finding.

Another important, albeit much less represented, group is that of community populations with social problems—the culturally deprived, school dropouts, and entire communities in need of resource aid. Child-centered, family-centered, and society-centered preventive programs are offered to these groups.

The changing picture of care-programs in mental health stands out vividly for both the mentally ill and essentially "normal" populations. Old roles will need to be redefined for nonprofessionals and professionals alike.

Manpower shortages, technological and social realities are breaking down the concentration of psychotherapeutic efforts for the middle and upper classes. This is not entirely without pitfalls; the danger exists that the nonprofessional will become the poor man's therapist.

We have begun to attempt ways to stem the tide of mental disorder as well as to treat the mentally ill. But we need to understand clearly what we aim to accomplish. (More than three-fourths of the experimental NIMH projects were primarily for the treatment of the chronically ill.)

A preventive index, developed in this research, may help us to refine our understanding of what we are doing in prevention. Mental hospitals can engage in primary prevention by skillful screening of applicants, particularly the aged poor who tend to be dumped into state hospitals not because they are mentally ill but because they are a nuisance to their families and communities. Geriatric centers which plan appropriate community home care and other types of care for the aged can do much to maximize hospital resources.

Increasingly, the term tertiary prevention will lose its euphemistic flavor as the hospital becomes more effective in rehabilitating the acutely and chronically ill. Attention will need to be focused very soon in the critical area of secondary prevention. Continued failure to spot early cases of disorder will wreak havoc in the nation's comprehensive prevention and treatment programs. A realistic, pragmatic approach, based on these realities and continuing evidence of nonprofessional abilities, will be required to guide mental health policy for some time to come.

Looking at the balance sheet, what else do we see to help us in planning? The youth of the nation, senior citizens, the "underprivileged," all minority ethnic groups, the "indigenous," the "hard-core unemployed," can be used more in mental health work than they have been. Clear evidence exists that retired persons over 65 are under-utilized as a group. Retired persons have great potential for understanding others in need and solving practical problems of living. Ease of recruiting the retired suggests that they readily perceive mental health service jobs as a way of combating boredom and enriching their lives. Revision of Social Security restrictions on earnings for the over-65 age group could greatly increase the manpower pool of paid nonprofessionals in mental health.

The young are vastly under-utilized even in experimental mental health projects. Limited use of adolescents as well as the over-65 age group is particularly important to correct in view of the increasing proportion of these two age groups in the American population. Exploration of human service careers should be encouraged early. Junior high schools and high schools should offer opportunity for young people to develop interest in understanding and helping people in need long before they are ready to enter the labor market. Youths of 15 and 16 can make substantial contributions to mental health by direct service to the mentally ill, to underprivileged groups, and indirectly, by infusing mental health organizations with a vitality and spontaneity which stimulates older workers, professionals and nonprofessionals.

Some unanticipated benefits may be accrued by planning for greater simultaneous use of older and younger citizens of the nation; a possible way of bridging the disturbing "generation gap" may be found. Training senior citizens side by side with teenagers and young adults in mental health service was reported by one project to create a climate of mutual understanding rarely found on the current social scene.

Not only age but also ethnic differences can be addressed. "College youth, tutoring potential minority-group candidates for college careers, can create a form of student power that lacks the heady illusion of instant utopia, but is a realistic way to improve society by means that respect everyone's rights."[1]

Some dent could be made in the high youth and minority unemployment figures if substantial numbers of unfilled jobs are filled from these groups, for these jobs are not being eliminated through automation. Selective experiments currently being undertaken in recruiting and training the "hard-core unemployed" by industry, with government sponsorship, might be considered for the mental health field. Survey responses indicate that underprivileged neighborhoods have considerable human resources.

In such neighborhoods, persons with little formal education have successfully served their neighbors, playing a catalytic role in group educational and therapeutic programs. Forty percent

---

[1] Editorial, *The New York Times*, May 22, 1968, "Discipline and Disruption." (Reference to disruptions at Columbia University Campus.)

of the projects attempted to recruit staffs defined as indigenous, but a still higher percentage found that more indigenous persons were employed in their projects than were actively sought. Former narcotic addicts, mental patients, alcoholics, have sufficiently aided themselves and fellow-sufferers to indicate the merit of continuing and intensifying this form of nonprofessional utilization.

More active emphasis on recruiting volunteers from the black and the white middle-class is another recommendation growing out of the 1968 NIMH Project Study. Affluence in itself does not lead to genuine participation in the mainstream of society. Financially privileged citizens of diverse ethnic groups should be encouraged to join the ranks of those who enrich their own lives by volunteering to help their communities and individual fellowmen in need. Yet, the "new" volunteer is also being sought from among the poor. Valuable experience can be gained from volunteering experience which is readily used to qualify an untrained person for a needed paid job in mental health.

EDUCATION OF NONPROFESSIONALS
AND PROFESSIONALS

Much is being written now about the need for continuing education and career lines for nonprofessionals beyond customary education. This is an essential first step in implementing recommendations for nonprofessional utilization. Future employers need not feel guilty about hiring nonprofessionals because the educational bureaucracies and the world of work will not credit their experience and allow them to move on to the next step of the mental health ladder.

Organizations such as the NIMH Continuing Education

183

Program of the Division of Manpower and Training have begun to address this problem by offering regular assistance in educating nonprofessionals at any public or private nonprofit institution. Career-lines on the high school level, through the community college and master's degree levels, are being developed by each of the core professional disciplines. Considering the breadth of functions being assumed by nonprofessionals, it is necessary to develop career lines in a broad framework—a community mental health framework which includes educators, social workers, psychiatrists, and others—rather than the separate conceptions of training current in curricula for nurses, social workers, psychologists, or psychiatrists working alone.

The ranks of the unskilled, untrained workers should be thinned by appropriate education and training programs. Hopefully, we will no longer require the term "nonprofessional" as precise titles—"community mental health worker" (trainee), social work associate, etc.—are appropriately designated and accepted. New professional groups—those of the mental health or community health professionals—will emerge from training programs which offer a master's or more advanced degree to those who ascend to the top of the mental health career ladder.

For professional education a key implication of this study is that a higher level of clinical, diagnostic, and treatment skill will be needed by the professional worker as he is relieved of some time-consuming tasks not requiring professional expertise. New skills as community educators and organizers have to be taught to professionals to help them to function in preventive community roles. Additional functions of training and supervising nonprofessionals in their special roles, featuring the constructive use of relationship, social therapy, and community interactional techniques, will need to be taken on by professionals in all mental health disciplines. The ability to teach basic concepts of human behavior on a level that is meaningful to persons of low education will become a crucial task for the future. The trend is clearly toward more common knowledge between professionals and nonprofessionals.

IMPLICATIONS FOR RESEARCH

Unsettled questions of nonprofessional utilization suggest that research is needed in many areas. Further research is suggested along the lines begun in this study; namely, clarification of the concept of levels of preventive intervention, and research efforts to operationalize "prevention" and "innovation" in mental health.

It is helpful for planners to learn precisely which level of prevention is receiving our greatest or least emphasis. Within each level it is also important to know exactly what is the nature of preventive goals and activities. For example, it was found in studying preventive index scores for each project that efforts devoted to providing alternatives to hospitalization, shortening hospital stays, and preventing rehospitalization raised preventive scores for projects which treated only the mentally ill. A high preventive index score usually meant that younger age groups were served, "normal" rather than diagnosed groups were cared for, and certain types of care and activities—for example, outpatient, community, and educational care—were given. Replication is needed to test this index and the validity of the five variables chosen to form the index.

Another research recommendation concerns a project's changing goals over time. It was observed that several projects which planned initially to focus on the treatment and rehabilitation of juvenile delinquents or drug addicts (tertiary prevention) moved to the goal of educating the public and developing community resources to help prevent juvenile delinquency or drug addiction (primary prevention).

185

We must become painfully objective and honest about why we alter our initial goals in mental health. Are we running from failure to treat difficult cases? Will we run from primary prevention back to treatment efforts when success in primary prevention appears dubious? The view that primary prevention is a more feasible and viable goal than tertiary prevention should be tested through systematic research. Study of specific barriers to goal achievement at different preventive levels—lack of a knowledge base, paucity of community resources, etc.—is urgently needed. Comparable experience must be evaluated so that we can explicate the various human and technical obstacles which stand in the way of achieving our national goals to prevent and to treat mental illness.

Research of a cross-disciplinary, epidemiological nature is also indicated to help us cope with the nation's mental health crisis. There is much to be learned about what predisposes us to mental and social breakdown. What are the characteristics of our high-risk populations in contrast to those of populations which appear to be less vulnerable to breakdown? Some of our favorite assumptions could stand rigorous testing.

Serious study of today's goals and delivery of services results in tomorrow's changed demands for service. Some types of service will be found wanting, and hopefully new patterns of service will be offered as these are discarded. Accordingly, the nonprofessional will need to keep pace with the changing reasons for his employment. Research, therefore, is indicated to study changing rationale for nonprofessional tasks and activities over time.

Evaluation of the nonprofessional's work also will be needed shortly. Although evaluative studies of professional functioning are still in their infancy, this in no way diminishes the point of assessing the performance of nonprofessionals, particularly in their newer functions.

Qualitative investigation of relations between professional and nonprofessional, especially in situations where nonprofessionals take on additional responsibilities, is also indicated. As discussed earlier in this chapter, and also in Chapter 2, changing ratios of nonprofessionals to professionals will affect interaction. Although this study produced evidence of a low ratio of nonprofessionals in community settings (in contrast to hospital settings), this pattern is changing. As the community realizes what the nonprofessional has to offer, increasing numbers will be employed in human-relationship, expediting, and educational roles. Well-planned study will be needed to evaluate the new interaction patterns which develop in answer to these changes.

RESEARCH ON THE "INDIGENOUS" WORKER

It is by now common knowledge that we have romanticized the indigenous worker, and that little hard data is available on the effect of employing and training this type of worker. No evidence exists of the indigenous worker's special knowledge or insight into his fellow man, nor is there evidence that he is necessarily motivated to help his fellow man more than the "socially distant" professional.

The indigenous worker is often better able to make contact with his fellow citizen because of familiarity with the language, customs, and life-style of his neighbors. However, it has been observed that in slum areas individuals are often locally bound simply because they lack the money to travel: their block is their community. Thus, we cannot expect a slum-dweller to have a broad understanding of life in his urban slum area.

Even if he did possess this understanding, he loses some of his "indigenity" the moment that he takes a job in the mental health establishment. He has already moved a step away from his neighbors, and presumably he will move still further away

187

to become a helper rather than a potential recipient of service.

What happens to the indigenous person in the course of the training process? Can he retain assets for which he was originally selected, or does he become socially distant like the typical professional? Many considerations need to be spelled out as we inquire into the effect of employing and training indigenous nonprofessionals.

Continued research to improve ways of blending many different levels of staff into one efficient operation is, indeed, a high priority. Chapter 2 refers to efforts to develop criteria for this task, but these efforts are clearly in an embryonic stage. Who does what part of the over-all mental health task is a question which deserves most careful research formulation.

One way to maximize our current experience with nonprofessionals for research use was found to be considerably neglected. Little systematic study of continued and subsequent employment of paid and volunteer nonprofessionals has been done. To plan intelligently for career lines, attention to the nonprofessionals' long-term employment patterns is vital. Follow-up of volunteers is also important, especially with the "new" volunteer who can use his experience to move into a job in the mental health opportunity structure. Many of our most successful lay planners in mental health were discovered to have begun their volunteer careers by giving direct service in mental health agencies in their communities.

IMPLICATIONS FOR MANPOWER AND MENTAL HEALTH THEORY

Manpower theory today is reported to be "a nebulous grouping of unsystematized conceptualizations." Too many facts of a social, demographic, economic, and psychological nature are

188

needed in order to be able to predict manpower needs. This knowledge is in a state of constant flux. To compound the difficulties, concepts of prevention and treatment in mental health are changing, as are the interrelationships between broad demographic and related mental health phenomena.

In a peacetime democratic nation, citizens must have considerable choice of where and at what they shall work. Their government should develop theory for the design of suitable manpower objectives with sufficient built-in incentives to channel manpower into such understaffed and significant areas as mental health. The study reported here suggests that the range of occupational alternatives for many Americans would be greatly enhanced by such measures as comprehensive recruitment programs, grants for education, and inservice training for nonprofessional personnel. All evidence points to the fact that the nation's intellectual and emotional resources are being tapped only partially in the service of the nation's mental health.

Emotional and social disturbances will be viewed increasingly as an inevitable response to the manifold problems of modern living that can best be rectified with vast social and educational programs involving society as a whole. The goals of our subject projects demonstrate that social change and social action goals are not incompatible with prevention and treatment. Indeed, these goals and the broad aim of encouraging citizen-participation can be planned in relation to specific levels of prevention and treatment.

As the public system of mental health care expands, need will increasingly be viewed as the only criterion for mental health care. This will come as a direct result of a new appreciation of civil rights and the rights of the poor. Although for some time various investigators have pointed out that existing prevention theory is not sufficiently defined, and that it has been difficult even to communicate about comparable experience, a beginning effort is made here to specify goals and the interrelationships among other variables considered significant to prevention. Refinement of prevention theory has been attempted in the hope that others will continue along this path, clarifying and defining prevention so that the nation can better plan comprehensive programs attending to the whole range of mental health and illness.

We need to look closely at some of our old assumptions about prevention efforts. It may be found, for example, that in the child-care field, which ideally should be the bastion of primary prevention, our institutions are set up primarily to cope with disintegrated families; hence, foster-care services are offered to pick up the pieces of families which fall apart under stress. But, to what extent are child-caring institutions focused on giving counsel and service to the average family before it succumbs to acute stress? Have we placed our most experienced workers at this front line of defense? The answer is, obviously, no. Even if the nonprofessional can aid in this job (and there is evidence to suggest that he may well be able to do so), the trained professional must first bring to this task his highest level of diagnostic knowledge. Heretofore we have reserved such skills for the mentally ill. The aim should be to consider many factors and promote mental health for all persons at all ages.

GUIDELINES FOR NONPROFESSIONAL UTILIZATION

At the beginning of the NIMH Study it was assumed that nonprofessionals were used either as an expedient (that is, resulting strictly from staff shortages) or because it was felt that they had a unique role to play which was not associated with professional performance. The following question, therefore, was posed in the survey: "In your opinion, are nonprofessionals being used chiefly in your project as an *expedient* because of staff shortages, or do you feel that they have a *unique* role?" Analysis of the responses to this question convinced us that this formulation was too simplistic, and that it should be dropped in favor of more dynamic considerations. Models which could take account of the way in which mental health service changes as persons with different types of background and training join the team began to be needed. In other words, a fresh look had to be taken at the whole question of nonprofessional utilization in order to understand more significant underlying factors.

In principle, all types of functions can be performed at all levels of prevention. Practically, however, certain task-patterns appear to lend themselves more readily to one or another preventive level. This type of knowledge, hopefully, would lead naturally to ideas for improving divisions of labor among different levels of personnel in the entire range of mental health settings.

Among the basic questions which should be asked in designing models for future nonprofessional utilization in mental health are: (1) Was a given task previously performed by professionals or is that task totally new to the mental health agency? (2) Is the task generally considered to require professional training? (3) Can the task be transferred simply to the nonprofessional (without change) or must it be redefined because it is to be performed by an untrained person?

If the answer to the first question is that the task is a new (or rediscovered) one which was not previously or recently performed by anyone, more than likely it is a task which does not require professional training. The popular "friendly companion" role performed by college student volunteers throughout this country falls into this category. The indigenous family planning

191

aide is another illustration of a more innovative task model essential to primary prevention. The industrial therapy aide, who works actively on the former mental patient's vocational adjustment after hospital discharge and reports back to the hospital professional staff, is another example at the tertiary preventive level. These tasks can be designated and tailored to fit the characteristics and attributes of available nonprofessional workers.

Where the task was one which was generally considered to require professional training, a hard look needs to be taken to ascertain that this remains a valid view. Many resource-finding functions, assumed by professional social workers to belong exclusively in their domain, are now being performed effectively by nonprofessionals. It is difficult to say that the job is being done in the same way when a nonprofessional handles it. Usually there is a subtle (or not so subtle) change based on knowledge and attitudinal differences between professionals and nonprofessionals.

On the other hand, there are many functions, rightly performed heretofore by professionals, which have had to be assigned to the nonprofessional for expedience. In such functions, the push toward task-reallocation was based strictly on staff shortages but the task was appropriately modified to safeguard performance. Many of the nonprofessionals fall into this category. The most common example is that of the large number of nonprofessionals conducting group therapy or engaging in milieu therapy. The occupational therapy aide, of course, is encouraged to use the skills he has already acquired when he moves into conducting activity group therapy for the mentally ill. Expectations of his performance are clearly less than those expected of a clinically trained professional conducting this type of therapy.

192

Indeed, there are tasks which can be transferred simply to the nonprofessional because these have never required professional training. Social work and nursing are two professional disciplines that have long been plagued by considerable routine, clerical aspects. Differential allocation of many caretaking, reception, and informational tasks should free professional staff of functions which never properly belonged in the professional province.

In the provision of treatment and rehabilitation for the severely mentally ill, nursing aides, social work "associates," and community mental health aides will continue to free professional staff in hospitals and clinics of traditional tasks not requiring their expertise. They will also be expected to continue to innovate with newer supportive tasks adapted to their highest potential abilities. In general, the vast reservoir of volunteer and paid manpower will be assigned to perform needed educational, expediting, and social supportive services to reach out to improve mental health in the community. Newly enlisted family planning aides, teacher aides, parent-education aides, and child-care aides will join the ranks of those whose eye is fixed on preventing or attending to the early signs of mental and social disorder.

These guidelines presuppose carefully tailored training programs and supervision to enable the nonprofessional to contribute to the interdisciplinary team. Models for supervision need to be examined carefully. Resistance to involving the nonprofessional needs to be eliminated.

To be effective, group counseling (currently a favored method in hospitals, clinics, in the corrections field, and in most mental health agencies) requires a certain minimum-experience level. Certain personality attributes and skills are needed, no matter how far group counseling moves from the classical psy-

193

choanalytic model. The same can be said for the interviewing tasks and dealing with "reality problems" which are considered roles of the nonprofessional mental health agent. The novice attempting social interventions in mental health learns very rapidly that there are few easy cases or problems. Even assignments of parts of problems present difficulty and challenge for the nonprofessional and the professional who delegates the assignment.

A very large order! But a bold and thoughtful innovative stance is the essential ingredient of the current revolution in mental and social health. As custodial care in mental hospitals recedes in importance, the citizen volunteer and the paid nonprofessional must move out into the community, become alert to the crisis of mental illness and to the daily crises of living for the entire community. New goals create new roles and tasks, and the implications for new manpower uses in mental health become enormous.

APPENDIX A

QUESTIONNAIRE OF SURVEY

DEPARTMENT OF HEALTH, EDUCATION, AND WELFARE
PUBLIC HEALTH SERVICE
National Institute of Mental Health

SURVEY OF N. I. M. H. PROJECT USE OF
NON-PROFESSIONAL STAFF IN MENTAL HEALTH FUNCTIONS

An N. I. M. H. Study Contracted to the Center for Research
and Demonstration
Columbia University School of Social Work

QUESTIONNAIRE OF SURVEY

SECTION A. GENERAL PROJECT INFORMATION

(See Instructions Pages 1-3)

1. TITLE OF N.I.M.H. PROJECT:

2. SPONSORING AGENCY (other than N.I.M.H.):

3. ADDRESS OF PROJECT:

    (Street No. or P.O. Box)   (City)   (State)   (Zip Code)

4. DURATION OF SERVICE OPERATION OF N.I.M.H. PROJECT: (See Instructions Page 3)

  a. Current Projects Only: b. Terminated Projects Only:

    Give length of time of service operation to date: Give total length of time of service operation:

    _____ _____   _____ _____

    Years Months   Years Months

5. PRIOR USE OF NONPROFESSIONALS IN SERVICE ROLES BY SPONSORING AGENCY: (See Instructions Page 3)

Has agency sponsoring N.I.M.H. project previously utilized nonprofessionals, paid or volunteer, to provide

direct services to pt./clients? Check One .... Yes _____ No _____ (If No is checked, go on to question 6)

If Yes, were nonprofessionals utilized in the following roles: Check ALL THAT APPLY for paid and volunteer staff.

                                    Paid   Volunteer

    a. Case Aides   _____ _____

    b. Nursing and Ward Personnel   _____ _____

    c. Recreational and Group Work Aides   _____ _____

    d. Homemakers   _____ _____

    e. Physical, Occupational, Vocational Rehab. Aides   _____ _____

    f. Other (Specify) _____   _____ _____

196

6. BASIS FOR UTILIZATION OF NONPROFESSIONAL PERSONNEL BY NIMH PROJECT (See Instructions Pages 3-4)

Note: Item 1 is concerned with certain characteristics of nonprofessional staff which may have been significant for your project. Items 2-5 emphasize possible bases for utilization of nonprofessional staff.
For ALL of the Items, CHECK those attributes or reasons which have been particularly RELEVANT for your project.

1. Attributes of Nonprofessional Staff:

_____ Better communication with patient/client group through shared communication style, or shared social characteristics.
_____ Knowledge of community resources, and how to "negotiate" them due to residence in same area.
_____ Understanding of specific problem or illness through direct experience with it.
_____ Reduction of social distance through nonprofessional status per se, whether or not above attributes also present.
_____ Other Special attributes (Specify) _____

2. For Extension of Service Programs:

_____ Reach out and involve client groups in need of project services.
_____ Provide caretaking services.
_____ Provide informal sustaining relationships to patients/clients.
_____ Promote client self-help through involving clients in helping others having same problems.
_____ Other extensions of service (Specify) _____

3. Promote Citizen Participation and Community Understanding:

_____ Increase general citizen participation in community service programs through stimulation of volunteer activity.
_____ Increase community understanding of mental health problems through stimulation of volunteer activity.
_____ Other community-focussed reasons (Specify) _____

4. Accommodation to Professional Manpower Shortage:

_____ Provide services which would be better provided by professional staff, if enough were available.
_____ Relieve professional staff of tasks not requiring professional expertise.
_____ Source of future recruitment of professional manpower for mental health services.
_____ Other accommodations (Specify) _____

5. Recruitment and Training of Nonprofessional Staff:

_____ Recruit and train persons not previously considered eligible for careers in human services field.
_____ Training for new service functions, or roles, for previously utilized nonprofessional staff.
_____ Other reasons related to nonprofessional staff (Specify) _____

197

7. INITIAL PROJECT GOALS (See Instructions Pages 5-6)

For EACH of the following goals (including Other, if applicable) please check the column which best indicates the amount of emphasis placed on the goal in planning your project.

PROJECT GOAL	AMOUNT OF EMPHASIS		
	Slight or None	Moderate	Essential or Strong
a. PROMOTE, PLAN and PROVIDE FOR GENERAL COMMUNITY MENTAL HEALTH: e.g., Housing, homemaker, pre-school programs; family life improvement programs; anticipatory counseling around childbirth, marriage, aging, etc.			
b. EARLY LOCATION, DIAGNOSIS AND TREATMENT OF SUS-PECTED AND/OR ACUTE DISTURBANCES TO WARD OFF MORE SERIOUS, LONG-TERM ILLNESS AND/OR ADJUSTMENT PROBLEMS (Exclude chronic cases). e.g. Screening and consultation services related to this goal; emergency walk-in clinic and partial hospitalization programs; all-time-limited programs, etc.			
c. PROVIDE TREATMENT AND/OR REHABILITATION TO LIMIT DISABILITIES AND FACILITATE COMMUNITY RETURN OF PERSONS WITH SEVERE AND CHRONIC ILLNESS AND/OR ADJUSTMENT PROBLEMS: e.g. Milieu therapy, half-way houses, foster homes or community-care residence for chronic patients, ex-pt. psychiatric social clubs, etc.			
d. PROMOTE CITIZEN PARTICIPATION AND SOCIAL ACTION IN THE COMMUNITY: e.g. stimulate parents to become active in schools, etc.			
e. Other goals: (Specify) _____			
_____			
_____			
_____			

198

SECTION B. DESCRIPTION OF NONPROFESSIONAL STAFF UTILIZED IN PROJECT (See Instructions pages 7-8)

For age and educational level, select appropriate number from Code.

For Each Category, please give in-formation requested. PAID non-professional staff category	No. Men	No. Women	AGE RANGES 1 (Under 18) 2 (18-21) 3 (22-64) 4 (Over 65)	EDUCATIONAL LEVEL 5 (Less than High Schl.) 6 (Some High School) 7 (High School Grad) 8 (Some College	ETHNIC COMP. (Name)	Average No. of Work- hours daily	Average no. of Work-days weekly
a. Case Aide							
b. Nursing and Ward Personnel							
c. Recreational and Group-work Aide							
d. Homemakers							
e. Physical, Occup., Voc.Rehab.Aides							
f. Other (Specify)							
VOLUNTEER nonprofessional staff category							
a. Case Aide							
b. Nursing and Ward Personnel							
c. Recreational and Group-work Aide							
d. Homemakers							
e. Physical, Occup., Voc.Rehab.Aides							
f. Other (Specify)							

199

2. OTHER CHARACTERISTICS OF NONPROFESSIONAL STAFF

How many of your PAID nonprofessional staff have had problems similar to pt./client group—e.g. ex-mental patient? Number _____

How many of your VOLUNTEERS have had problems/illness similar to pt./client group?..........Number _____

Are there any other similar social characteristics between nonprofessional staff and patient/client group? (Check one) ....Yes _____ No _____
    If Yes, specify and give staff category, indicating whether paid or volunteer _____

Page 4

SECTION C. INFORMATION ON PROJECT PROFESSIONAL STAFF

(See Instructions Pages 8-9)

1. Professional Disciplines Associated with Project

Percent of Professional Time ALLOCATED to:
(Please give the most reasonable estimate possible)

Professional Disciplines Associated with Project	CHECK ALL RELE- VANT	No. Employed by Project		Training of Non- prof. Staff	Superv. of Non- prof. Staff	Admin. of Proj.	Re- search	Superv. of Prof. Staff	Direct Services to Pat./ Clients	Services to Com- munity	Other (Specify)
		FULL TIME	PART TIME								
a. Psychiatrists											
b. Other Physicians											
c. Psychologists											
d. Social Workers											
e. Registered Nurses											
f. Teachers											
g. Sociologists/ Anthropologists											
h. Occupational Therapists											
i. Other Pro- fessional Staff (Specify)											

2. If time is given by professional staff to "services to community," please indicate the nature of these services -- e.g. consultation to community agencies, etc. _____

_____

200

Page 5

SECTION D. NATURE OF PROJECT POPULATION (See instructions pages 10-11)

For ages and educational level, select appropriate number from code.

1. Diagnostic and Other Groups Served / Give for Each Group Served, all characteristics that apply to the majority of the group.	SEX (Check) Men	Women	AGE RANGES 0 (Birth to 5 yrs.) 1 (6-11 yrs.) 2 (12-17 yrs.) 3 (18-64 yrs.) 4 (65 and over)	EDUCATIONAL LEVEL 5 (Less than High Schl.) 6 (High School Grad) 7 (Some College)	ETHNIC COMP. (Name)	Other Significant Characteristics (Specify)
a. Mentally Ill						
b. Alcoholics						
c. Drug Addicts						
d. Adjudged delinquency and offenders						
e. Underprivileged						
f. Age-group problems						
g. School drop-outs						
h. Other (Specify)						

2. If mentally ill group is served, check here if mainly acute _____, mainly chronic _____, both acute and chronic _____.

3. Is project attempting to reach groups which sponsoring agency has not previously served? Yes ____ No ____ If Yes, name _____

4. How many people received project service in a representative month? (See Instructions Page 11) Give Total No. _____
(Month: _____)

Service given: To Individuals Only? _____ ; In Small Groups Only? _____ ; Ind. and Small Groups _____
(No.) (No.) (No.)

Does Project conduct large group community meetings? Yes ____ No ____ ; if YES, give average attendance
(Check)
per meeting _____.

201

SECTION E. SERVICE TO PROJECT POPULATION (See instructions page 12)

1. Types of Care Provided by Project

Which type of care does your Project provide to the problem-groups served? (Refer to groups checked on page 6, Question 1) Check ALL that apply and specify group(s) served.

(Check)	Type of Care	Group Served	Check	Type of Care	Group Served
a.	In-patient		e.	Foster family care	
b.	Out-patient		f.	Care in own home	
c.	Day or Night Hosp.		g.	Social agency care	
d.	Half-way house		h.	Other (Name)	

Name TYPES OF CARE if checked, which were NOT previously provided by sponsoring agency. _____

2. HOURS OF PROJECT OPERATION and AVAILABILITY OF STAFF (See Instructions Page 12)

CHECK Availability of Project Professional and Nonprofessional Staff for Project's Hours of Operation:

Hours Project in Operation	Professional Staff Available		PAID Non-professionals Available		VOLUNTEER Non-professionals Available	
	Reg.	On Call	Reg.	On Call	Reg.	On Call
a. Mon.-Fri., 9AM - 5 PM Only						
b. Day and Evening Hours - NO Weekends						
c. During Days and Weekends - NO Evenings						
d. 24 Hour Service - 7 days a week						
e. Other schedule (please specify)						

	Case-Aide		Nursing and Ward Personnel		Recreat. Group-work aide		Home-makers		Phys. Occup. Voc. Rehab.		Other Titles 1.		Other Titles 2.		Performed ALSO by Prof. Staff (Check)
	Pd.	Vol.	Pd.	Vol.	Pd.	Vol.	Pd.	Vol.	Pd.	Vol.	Pd.	Vol.	Pd.	Vol.	
1. Case-finding and facilitation of access to project services															
2. Reception Orientation to Service															
3. Screening (non-clerical)															
4. Caretaking—e.g. ward-care, day care															
5. Therapeutic Functions:															
a. Individual counseling															
b. Group counseling															
c. Socializing relationships (Individual or group)															
d. Activity–group therapy															
e. Milieu therapy															
f. Other therapeutic functions Name															
6. Special Skill Functions:															
a. Tutoring															
b. Retraining--Specify types															
c. Other special skills (Specify)															
7. Adjustment to Community:															
a. Resource-finding--e.g. home, job															
b. Facilitate access to community services															
c. Other (Specify)															
8. Community Improvement (Specify)															
9. Other Functions (Specify)															

203

Page 8

10. Were any of the functions checked as performed by BOTH professional and nonprofessional staff performed:

Check one

EQUALLY by both _____ Which functions? _____

MAINLY by nonprofessionals _____ Which functions? _____

MAINLY by professionals _____ Which functions? _____

11. Is project attempting to have nonprofessionals perform functions which sponsoring agency has not previously provided? Check one Yes_____ No_____ (If No, go to question 12.)

If YES, state function(s) and who performs them (paid or volunteer) _____

12. Are any specialized techniques being used in performance of the above functions by nonprofessionals?

Check one: Yes _____ No _____ If YES: a.) For which functions? _____

b.) By whom? (Please give category--paid and/or vol.) _____

204

SECTION F. RECRUITMENT, TRAINING, AND SUPERVISION (See instructions, page 13)

1. METHODS OF RECRUITMENT UTILIZED

	Check ALL Used	CHECK To Whom Applicable			Rate the EFFECTIVENESS of EACH Method Used: Check ONE			
		Both Paid and Volunteer	Primarily Paid Staff	Primarily Volunteer Staff	Very Effect.	Mod. Effect.	Slightly Effect.	Not Effect.
a. Local Employment Agencies								
b. Recommendation by Nonprofessionals								
c. Recommendation by Project Professionals								
d. Group Meetings for Prospective applicants								
e. Advertisements in News Media, posters, etc.								
f. Talks to Community Volunteer and other groups								
g. Other (Specify)								

1.1 Did you attempt to recruit any special types of groups as nonprofessionals, e.g., housewives, retired people, college students? Please Check One:................. Yes___ No___
If Yes, specify type of group, and whether as paid or volunteer staff: _____

1.2 Did you attempt to recruit nonprofessionals having the same social characteristics as your patient/client group, e.g., Similar nationality, racial, religious or class background; or coming from the same neighborhood, etc. Please Check One .... Yes___ No___

If YES, specify: _____

1.3 Did you use any particular screening methods in recruiting nonprofessional staff, paid and/or volunteer? Please Check One:.................. Yes___ No___
If Yes, describe the methods used and indicate whether primarily for paid and/or volunteer staff, or particular category, if applicable: _____

205

2. PROBLEMS IN RECRUITMENT

A. Have there been problems in recruiting nonprofessional staff, either Paid or Volunteer, or both? Check ONE. Yes _____ No _____
(If Yes, go on to question B; if No, go on to question 3.)

B.

PROBLEMS IN RECRUITMENT	For EACH Relevant Problem, CHECK Appropriate Staff Category		
	Both Paid and Volunteers	Primarily Paid Staff	Primarily Volunteer Staff
1. Situational Factors:			
a. Transportation to project			
b. Scheduling of hours of work, e.g., evenings/weekends			
c. Other (Specify) _____			
2. Personnel Arrangements:			
a. Low wage/salary levels			
b. Little chance of promotion			
c. No Reimbursement for expenses related to work			
d. Inadequate Physical Facilities			
e. Other (Specify) _____			
3. Qualifications of Nonprofessionals:			
a. Age: Applicants too young			
Applicants too old			
b. Sex: Too few male applicants			
Too few female applicants			
c. Education: Insufficient			
Over–educated			
d. Discomfort re: Problems/Illness of Groups Served by project			
e. Difficulty in Locating Persons with Needed Skills and Aptitudes			
f. Other (Specify) _____			
4. General Lack of Response to Recruitment Efforts			

206

CATEGORY OF NON-PROFESSIONAL STAFF	Include ONLY Training AFTER Orientation to Project – Otherwise LEAVE BLANK TYPE OF TRAINING: CHECK ALL APPLICABLE			Give Length of Time of Training Period in Days, or Months	SUPERVISION AVAILABLE TO CATEGORY: CHECK ONE		
ALL Paid Titles	Didactic Courses, Lectures, Films, etc.	On-job, Apprentice Training, Observation, etc.	Other (Specify) ___		Regul. Avail.	Occas. Avail.	Only if Emergency arises
a. Case Aide							
b. Nursing and Ward Personnel							
c. Recreational and Group-Work Aide							
d. Homemakers							
e. Physical, Occup., Voc. Rehab Aides							
f. Other (Specify) ___							
ALL Volunteer Titles							
a. Case Aide							
b. Nursing and Ward Personnel							
c. Recreational and Group-work aide							
e. Physical, Occup., Voc. Rehab. Aides							
f. Other (Specify) ___							

DESCRIBE IF ANY SPECIAL TRAINING METHOD, TYPE OF SUPERVISION WAS INSTITUTED, etc. FOR ANY OF THE CATEGORIES, PAID OR VOLUNTEER AND SPECIFY CATEGORY: _____

_____

_____

SECTION G.   ASSESSMENT OF USE OF NONPROFESSIONAL STAFF   (See Instructions pages 14-15)

1.   PROJECT GOALS ACHIEVED AND CONTRIBUTION OF NONPROFESSIONAL STAFF

GOALS OF PROJECT	Check if Relevant to Project	DEGREE OF ACHIEVEMENT OF GOAL: CHECK ONE			CONTRIBUTION OF NONPROFESSIONAL STAFF TO GOAL ACHIEVEMENT CHECK ONE		
		Fully	Moderately	Slightly or not at all	Substantial	Moderate	Little or None
a. PROMOTE, PLAN and PROVIDE FOR GENERAL COMMUNITY MENTAL HEALTH							
b. EARLY LOCATION, DIAGNOSIS AND TREATMENT OF SUSPECTED AND/OR ACUTE DISTURBANCES TO WARD OFF MORE SERIOUS, LONG-TERM ILLNESS AND/OR ADJUSTMENT PROBLEMS							
c. PROVIDE TREATMENT AND/OR REHABILITATION TO LIMIT DISABILITIES AND FACILITATE COMMUNITY RETURN OF PERSONS WITH SEVERE AND CHRONIC ILLNESS AND/OR ADJUSTMENT PROBLEMS							
d. PROMOTE CITIZEN PARTICIPATION AND SOCIAL ACTION IN THE COMMUNITY							
e. Other (Specify) _____							

2.   SUGGESTED CHANGES RE: UTILIZATION OF NONPROFESSIONAL STAFF

Indicate CHANGES, if any, you would suggest in SELECTION, TRAINING, SUPERVISION and TASK ASSIGNMENT for nonprofessional staff, both paid and volunteer, based on your experience: _____

_____

_____

_____

208

3. NONPROFESSIONAL CONTRIBUTION TO IMPROVEMENTS IN SERVICE TO PROJECT POPULATION

If any of the listed improvements occurred in your project, CHECK the ONE column which best describes the degree of nonprofessional contribution to the improved service(s).

IMPROVEMENTS IN SERVICE	DEGREE OF NONPROFESSIONAL CONTRIBUTION			
	Substantial	Moderate	Slight	Not at all
a. Services Initiated and Completed Faster				
b. Able to serve More People				
c. New Services Provided				
d. More Professional Time Made Available for Treatment				
e. New viewpoints gained by project staff re: population served				
f. Other (Specify) _____				
_____				
_____				

4. SERVICE JUSTIFICATION

a. In your opinion, does the service performed by nonprofessionals justify the expense of training, supervision, and general agency overhead?
Check One

For Paid Nonprofessionals   Yes _____   No _____

For Volunteer Nonprofessionals   Yes _____   No _____

b. In your opinion, are nonprofessionals being used chiefly in your project as an expedient because of staff shortages, or do you feel that they have a unique role?

CHECK ONE: EXPEDIENT _____   UNIQUE ROLE _____

Page 14

209

5. INTERACTION OF PROFESSIONAL–NONPROFESSIONAL STAFF

The following are some of the advantages and disadvantages of collaboration between professionals and non-professionals. CHECK for Paid and Volunteer staff ALL that were relevant for your project.

	APPLIES TO		PARTICULAR CATEGORY OF NONPROFESSIONAL (Name)
	Paid	Vol. Staff	
a. Provides experience in supervision for professional staff.			
b. Overlapping of functions between professionals and nonprofessionals.			
c. Expanded professional staff's understanding of client-group association with nonprofessionals.			
d. Required additional professional time for training and supervision.			
e. Caused communication problems.			
f. Status competition between the two groups.			
g. Other (Specify)			

For those problems checked above, DESCRIBE any attempts which proved SUCCESSFUL in reducing interaction problems:

6. OBSTACLES TO EMPLOYMENT BY SPONSORING AGENCY

Is there any obstacle in the administrative-personnel system governing your sponsoring agency which would interfere with hiring successfully trained non-professionals from your project?

Check One: No Obstacles_____ Some delay or difficulty_____ Impossible_____

210

Let us suppose that professional staff and monies became available during the course of your project. Would you have preferred to utilize them rather than continuing to work with your non-professional staff who are performing functions which professionals previously performed? CHECK ONLY ONE

_____ Would clearly utilize Professional Staff

_____ Probably would utilize professional staff

_____ Uncertain

_____ Probably not utilize professional staff

_____ Clearly not utilize professional staff

(Respondents for Current Projects, please skip to "Additional Comments" Page 17.)

SECTION H. FOR TERMINATED PROJECTS

These questions are addressed only to terminated projects, i.e., projects for whom funding by NIMH has terminated at this time.

1. OUTCOME OF TERMINATED PROJECTS

The following is a list of possible outcomes of terminated projects. PLEASE CHECK ONE.

_____ Project completely discontinued at termination.

_____ Project became part of ongoing program of sponsoring agency.

_____ Project became part of ongoing program of another agency in the community. (Specify)

_____ Other outcome (Specify) _____

_____

2. Did utilization of non-professionals in the project result in any changes in the TABLES of PERSONNEL ORGANIZATION of the agency? Check One: Yes _____ No _____

If Yes, please specify changes: _____

_____

211

3. CAREER OUTCOMES FOR NONPROFESSIONALS

Would you please CHECK the appropriate career outcomes of nonprofessional staff since termination of your project? For those CHECKED, please give Number of Staff for Paid and/or Volunteer, if known, and particular category, if applicable.

		NO. OF STAFF		CATEGORY
Check		Paid	Vol.	
Working at the sponsoring agency in the same capacity.		___	___	___
Working at the sponsoring agency in a different capacity.		___	___	___
Working at another community agency in the mental health field.		___	___	___
Employed in a different field of work.		___	___	___
Unknown outcome.		___	___	___
Other (Specify) ___		___	___	___
___				___

ADDITIONAL COMMENTS

We would appreciate any further comments you may have on the utilization of nonprofessional personnel. Thank you for your cooperation in filling out this questionnaire.

_____

_____

_____

NAME OF RESPONDENT: _____

(Note: If respondent is/was not project director, please indicate under Title)

TITLE: _____

PROFESSIONAL DISCIPLINE: _____

DATE OF RESPONSE: _____

APPENDIX B

INSTRUCTIONS TO SCORERS
OF INDIVIDUAL QUESTIONNAIRES

I. PREVENTION INDEX SCORE
(Based on cumulative weighted scores)

Item 1

| | Goal Patterns | |
Goal Patterns	Rating	Score
1	High	3
2	High	3
3	Medium	2
4	Medium	2
5	Low	1
6	High	3

Item 2

Project Population—Diagnosed or Not Diagnosed
(Nominal Scale—not a continuum)

Score

I. *Diagnosed population only,* consisting of:
    a. Mentally Ill
    b. Alcoholics   1
    c. Drug Addicts
    d. Adjudged Delinquents
II. *Nondiagnosed population only or both,* consisting of:
    e. Underprivileged
    f. Age Group Problems
    g. School Dropouts   3
    h. Other

Select Highest Score.

Item 3

Project Population—Age Group[1]

Age Group	Rating	Score
Children 0-11	High	3
Adolescents 12-17	Medium	2
Adults 18-64	Low	1

---

[1] If more than one age group is served, select the score which is highest, i.e., if Adults and Adolescents and Children are served, select score 3.

Item 4[2]   *Selected Professional and Nonprofessional Activities*

Activity	Score Breakdown	
10% or more time in services to community	1	
Certain Professional Services to Community		
a. Specific educational program or other specific preventive program, e.g. family life education	2	Select the Highest
b. Consultation, community planning and organization, referrals	1	
Large Community Meetings		
Certain Nonprofessional Activities if specified:		
Casefinding, Community Improvement, Reality Counseling, Crisis Intervention, tutoring, alcoholism counseling, retraining	1 for 1 function 2 for 2 or more functions Select Highest	

[2] Note that the total highest score for Item 4 is 6. This, however, is a temporary score. Please convert the temporary score to the final score for this item using the following reduction table:

Temporary Score	Final Score	Rating
1 or 2	1	Low
3 or 4	2	Medium
5 or 6	3	High

Item 5

Total Institutional Care or Not

Type of Care	Rating	Score
Traditional hospital inpatient care *only*	Low	1
Clinic and Hospital Care—day hospital, Halfway House	Medium	2
Other Community Care —e.g. home care, educational, etc.	High	3

Select highest, in case of both in-patient care and other care.

II. COMPONENTS OF THE INNOVATION INDEX SCORE

Item Description (As stated in questionnaire)

Has agency previously used non-professionals?*

Reach out and involve client groups in need for project services.

Under *other extensions*: Provide a needed service that did not exist previously.

Under *Other community-focussed reasons*:

Create potential employment resources;
Develop leadership in the community;
Bridge between community agencies and neighborhood of project.

---

* Only this first item received a 2-point score. All other items received one point. See text, Chapt. VII, for explanation.

216

Recruit and train persons *not* previously considered eligible for careers in human services.

Training for *new* service functions or roles for previously utilized nonprofessionals.

Attempt to reach groups which sponsoring agency had not previously served.

Name types of care if checked which were *not* previously given, by agency.

Is project attempting to have nonprofessionals perform functions *not* previously given?

Did you attempt to recruit any *special* types of groups as non-professionals?

SELECTED BIBLIOGRAPHY

Albee, G. W. *Mental Health Manpower Trends*. New York: Basic Books, 1961.

—— "The Manpower Crisis in Mental Health." Vol. 50, No. 12, *American Journal of Public Health*, Dec. 1960, 1895-1900.

—— "Needed: A Conceptual Breakthrough." *Mental Health Manpower,* Vol. I of a Mental Health Planning Study of Calif. Dep't of Mental Hygiene, prepared by M. Klutch. 2 vols. Calif., June 1967.

Alexander, H. L., W. Clausen. *Exploration in Social Psychiatry*. New York: Basic Books, 1957.

American Psychiatric Association. *The Volunteer and the Psychiatric Patient*, Report of Conference on Volunteer Services to Psychiatric Patients. Chicago, Ill. June 12-17, 1958 and Washington, D.C., 1959.

American Public Health Association Inc. *Mental Disorders: A Guide to Control Methods*, 1962.

Anderson, D. M., and J. M. Dockhorn. "Differential Use of Staff: An Exploration with Job-Trained Personnel." *Personnel Information*, New York: National Association of Social Workers, 1965.

Arkansas Rehabilitation Research and Training Center, and Association of Rehabilitation Centers, Inc. *Selection, Training, and Utilization of Supportive Personnel in Rehabilitation Facilities*, Report of Conference. Hot Springs, Arkansas. Sept., 1966.

Atkinson, Paula. "Alternative Career Opportunities for Neighborhood Workers." *Social Work*, Vol. 12, No. 4, Oct. 1967, pp. 81-88.

Baker, M. R. "Approaches to a Differential Use of Staff." *Social Casework,* April 1966, pp. 228-33.

Barber, Bernard. "Bureaucratic Organization and the Volunteer." *Social Perspectives on Behavior,* ed. Herman Stein and R. Cloward, Free Press of Glencoe, pp. 606-9.

Barker, Robert L., and Thomas L. Briggs. *Differential Use of Social Work Manpower.* New York: National Association of Social Workers, 1968.

Beck, B. *Prevention and Treatment.* N.A.S.W. Commission on Social Work Practice (based on work of the Subcommittee on Trends, Issues and Priorities), 1959. (mimeographed).

Beck, James C., David Kantor, and Victor A. Gelineau. "Follow-up Study of Chronic and Psychotic Patients 'treated' by College Case-Aid Volunteers." *American Journal of Psychiatry,* Vol. 120, No. 3, pp. 269-71.

Bellak, L. *Handbook of Community Psychiatry and Community Mental Health.* New York: Grune & Stratton, 1964.

Black, Bertram J. "Comprehensive Community Mental Health Services: Setting Social Policy." *Social Work,* Jan. 1967, National Association of Social Workers, pp. 51-58.

Blain, Daniel. "The Use of People in Mental Health Activities." *Mental Health Manpower,* Vol. II of a Mental Health Planning Study of Calif. Dep't of Mental Hygiene, prepared by M. Klutch, 2 vols., California, June 1967.

Boehm, W. W. "The Nature of Social Work." *Social Work,* III, 2:10-18, 1958.

Bower, Eli, M. "Primary Prevention of Mental and Emotional Disorders; A Conceptual Framework and Action Possibilities." *American Journal of Orthopsychiatry,* Vol. 33, No. 5, Oct. 1963, pp. 832-48.

Bowlby, John. *Maternal Care and Mental Health.* World Health Organization, (Geneva), Second Edit., Monograph Series No. 2, 1952.

Brager, G. "The Indigenous Worker: A New Approach for the Social Work Technician." *Social Work,* April 1965, pp. 33-40.

220

Buell, B. *Community Planning for Human Services.* New York: Columbia University Press, 1952.

Buell, B. et al. "Reorganizing to Prevent and Control Disordered Behavior." *Mental Hygiene,* XLII, April 1958, pp. 155-94.

Caplan, Gerald. *An Approach to Community Mental Health.* Grune & Stratton, 1961.

——— *Mental Health Aspects of Social Work in Public Health.* U.S. Dept. of Health, Educ. & Welfare, Washington, D.C., 1956.

——— *Principles of Preventive Psychiatry.* New York: Basic Books, 1964.

——— *Concepts of Mental Health and Consultation.* Children's Bureau Pub. No. 373, Washington, D.C.: Govt. Printing Office, 1959.

Cavanaugh, Joseph. "Mental Health Manpower Research." *Mental Health Manpower,* Volume II, Calif. Dep't of Mental Hygiene, June 1967.

Center for Youth and Community Studies. "Training Reports." Community Apprentice Program. Washington, D.C.: Howard University, 1964 and 1965.

Chaplan, A. A., John M. Price, I. Zuckerman, and Jon Ek. "The Role of Volunteers in Community Mental Health Programs." Community Mental Health Journal, Vol. 2, #3, Fall 1966, pp. 255-58.

Cloward, Richard, and Frances Piven. "Politics, Professionalism and Poverty." Arden House Conference on The Role of Government in Promoting Social Change. Harriman, New York, 1965.

Conant, J. B. *Slums and Suburbs.* Signet Book, 1964.

Costin, Lela. "Training Non-Professionals for a Child Welfare Service." *Children,* Vol. 13, No. 2, March 1966, pp. 63-68.

Council on Social Work Education. "The Manpower Crisis." (Bimonthly News Publication, Dec. 1964-Jan. 1965.)

Cowen, E. L., E. A. Gardner, and M. Zax. *Emergent Approaches to Mental Health Problems.* New York: Appleton-Century-Crofts, 1967.

221

Cumming, Elaine, and John Cumming. *Closed Ranks.* Cambridge, Mass.: Harvard University Press, 1946.

——— *Ego and Milieu,* New York: Atherton Press, 1962.

Davis, Kingsley. "Mental Hygiene and the Class Structure." *Psychiatry,* 1:55-56, 1938.

Delliquadri, F. P. "The New Block (or Bottleneck) to Recruitment." *Social Work Education.* New York: Council on Social Work Education, Dec. 1964-Jan. 1965.

Deutschle, K. W. "Organizing Preventive Health Programs to Meet Health Needs." Annals of the American Academy of Political and Social Science, Phila., Pa., Sept. 1961.

Dubos, R. *Mirage of Health,* New York: Harper, 1959, pp. 86-87.

Duhl, L. J. *The Urban Condition.* New York: Basic Books, 1963.

Edwards, Allen. *Techniques of Attitude Scale Construction.* New York: Appleton-Century-Crofts, 1957, p. 151.

Eliasoph, Eugene. "The Use of Volunteers as Case Aides in a Treatment Setting." *Social Casework,* Vol. 40, March 1959, pp. 141-44.

Elinson, Jack, Elena Padilla, and Marvin E. Perkins. *Public Image of Mental Health Services.* Mental Health Materials Center, Inc., New York, 1967.

Encyclopedia of Social Work, H. L. Lurie, Editor. National Association of Social Workers, New York, 1965.

Erikson, Erik. *Childhood and Society.* W. W. Norton & Co., Inc., New York, 1963.

——— *Identity and the Life Cycle,* Monograph 1, Psychological Issues, Vol. I, No. 1. New York: International Universities Press, 1959.

Farrar, M., and M. L. Hemmy. "Use of Non-Professional Staff in Work With the Aged." *Social Work,* pp. 44-50, July 1963.

Felix, R. "The National Mental Health Program." *American Journal of Public Health,* pp. 1804-1809, Nov. 1964.

Fenichel, Carl. "Mama or M.A.?: The 'Teacher-Mom' Program Evaluated." Reprint from Vol. 1, No. 1 of the *Journal of Special Education,* 1966.

Finestone, S. "Concepts of Staff Development and Impact of Institutional Environment." *Staff Development in Mental Health Services,* eds. Magner, George, and Thomas Briggs. National Association of Social Workers, New York, 1966.

——— Differential Utilization of Casework Staff in Public Welfare: Major Dimensions., Mimeogr. paper, May 1964.

——— "Strategies for Research in Public Welfare Administration." *Social Work Practice,* 1964. New York: National Conference on Social Welfare, 1964.

Fishman, J. R., A. Pearl, and B. MacLennan. "New Careers: Ways Out of Poverty for Disadvantaged Youth." Report of Conference Sponsored by Howard Univ. Center for Youth and Community Studies, Washington, D.C., March 1965.

Galloway, James, and Robert Kelso. "Don't Handcuff the Aide." *Rehabilitation Record,* March-April 1966, Vol. 7, No. 2, pp. 1-3.

Ginsberg, Eli. *A Policy for Scientific and Professional Manpower.* The National Manpower Council. New York: Columbia University Press, 1953.

Goffman, E. *On the Characteristics of Total Institutions and Asylums.* New York: Doubleday and Co., 1961.

Goldman, Alfred E., and M. Powell Lawton. "The Role of the Psychiatric Aide." *Mental Hygiene,* XLIV, No. 2, 1962, pp. 288-98.

Gordon, J. "Project Cause: The Federal Anti-Poverty Program and Some Implications of Sub-Professional Training." *American Psychologist,* Vol. 20, No. 5, May 1965.

Greenfield, Harry I, and Carol Brown. *Allied Health Manpower: Trends & Prospects.* New York: Columbia University Press, 1969.

Greenwood, E. "Attributes of a Profession." *Social Work,* July 1957, pp. 45-55.

Gurin, E. et al. *Americans View Their Mental Health.* Joint Commission on Mental Illness and Health, Monograph Series No. 4, New York: Basic Books, 1960.

Harrington, Michael. *The Other America.* Baltimore: Penguin Books, 1963.

Heyman, M. "Criteria for the Allocation of Cases According to Levels of Staff Skill." *Social Casework,* July 1961, pp. 325-31.

Hollingshead, A. B., and F. C. Redlich. *Social Class and Mental Illness: A Community Study.* J. Wiley and Sons, 1958.

Hollis, F. "Contemporary Issues for Caseworkers." In *Ego Oriented Casework: Problems and Perspectives.* New York: Family Service Association of America, 1963, pp. 6-15.

———— "A Profile of Early Interviews in Marital Counseling." *Social Casework,* Jan. 1968, pp. 35-43.

Huessy, Hans, R. *Mental Health with Limited Resources: Yankee Ingenuity in Low-Cost Programs.* New York and London: Grune and Stratton, 1966.

Jahoda, Marie. *Current Concepts of Positive Mental Health.* New York: Basic Books, 1958.

James, George. "A Chronicle of Progress." *Public Health Report,* Vol. 80, No. 2, Feb. 1965, pp. 96-98.

Janis, I. L. 'Emotional inoculation: theory and research on effects of preparatory communications." In *Psychoanalysis and the Social Sciences,* eds. Muensterberger and Axelrad. New York, International Universities Press, 1958. Vol. 5, pp. 119-54.

Joint Commission on Mental Illness and Health. *Action for Mental Health.* New York: Basic Books, 1961.

Jones, Betty Lacy. *Nonprofessional Workers in Professional Foster Family Agencies.* University of Pennsylvania School of Social Work, D.S.W., University Microfilms, Inc. Ann Arbor, Michigan, 1966.

Jones, Maxwell. *The Therapeutic Community.* Basic Books, 1953.

Kadushin, A. "Introduction of New Orientations in Child Welfare Research." In *The Known and Unknown in Child Welfare Research: An Appraisal.* Norris & Wallace, New York Child Welfare League of America and National Association of Social Workers, 1965, pp. 28-39.

Kahn, A. J. "The Societal Context of Social Work Practice." *Social Work,* October 1965.

———— "The Function of Social Work in the Modern World." *Issues in American Social Work.* New York: Columbia University Press, 1959.

———— *Planning Community Services for Children in Trouble,* New York: Columbia University Press, 1964.

———— Exploratory Essays in Social Welfare Planning, (Unpublished). New York: Columbia University School of Social Work Library, mimeo 1962.

———— Planning and Practice Perspectives on the Boundaries of Community Psychiatry. Paper presented in Conference on Community Psychiatry, U. of Wisconsin, Madison: June 18, 1964.

Kahn, Herman. *The Year 2000.* Macmillan and Co., 1967.

Kantrowitz, Nathan, and Donnell M. Papperfort. "Social Statistics for Metropolitan New York," No. 2, compiled at the School of Social Work of Columbia University, March 1966.

Kaplan, D. M., and E. A. Mason. "Maternal Reactions to Premature Birth Viewed as an Acute Emotional Disorder." *American Journal of Orthopsychiatry,* 30:539-46, July 1960.

Karowe, Harris. "How Volunteers can Help Disadvantaged Children." *Children,* July/August, 1967, pp. 151-55.

Kelley, James G. The mental health agent in the urban community. In *Urban America and the planning of mental health services.* New York: Group for Advancement of Psychiatry, 1964, pp. 474-94.

Kennedy, J. F. Message From the President of the United States Relating to Mental Illness and Mental Retardation. Feb. 5, 1963. 88th Congress, First Session, House of Representatives, Document No. 58.

Klein, William L. "The Training of Human Service Aides" in *Emergent Approaches to Mental Health.* New York: Appleton-Century-Crofts, 1967, pp. 158-61.

Leavell, H. R., and E. G. Clark. *Preventive Medicine for the Doctor in his Community.* New York: McGraw-Hill, 1968.

Levenson, Alan I., Bertram S. Brown, and Ruth I. Knee. "The Joint

225

Role of Public and Private Hospitals in Community Mental Health." In *Hospitals, Journal of the American Hospital Association*, Vol. 42, 1968, pp. 12-16.

Levine, Eugene. "Nursing Staffing in Hospitals." *The American Journal of Nursing*, Vol. 61, No. 9, Sept. 1961.

Levine, Eugene, Stanley E. Siegel, and Arnold Testoff. "Analysis of Part-time Nursing in General Hospitals. *Hospitals, Journal of the American Hospitals Association*, Vol. 37, No. 17, Sept. 1963.

Levine, Morton. "Trends in Professional Employment." *Manpower in Social Welfare*, edited by Edward Schwartz. New York: National Association of Social Workers, 1966.

Levinson, P., and J. Schiller. "Role Analysis of the Indigenous Non-Professional." *Social Work*, Vol. 2, No. 3, July 1966.

Lewin, Kurt. "Forces behind Food Habits and Methods of Change." Bulletin of the *National Research Council*, 1943, 108, pp. 35-65.

Lindemann, E. "Symptomatology and Management of Acute Grief." *American Journal of Psychiatry*, 101:141-48, 1944.

Lippitt, R., J. Watson, and B. Westley. *The Dynamics of Planned Change*. New York: Harcourt, Brace and Co., 1958.

Loomis, C. P. *Social Systems: Essays on Their Persistence and Change*. Princeton, N. J.: D. Van Nostrand Co., 1960.

Medical Tribune and Medical News, March 11, 1968, April 22, 1968. New York: Medical Tribune, Inc.

Mental Health Education: A Critique. Pennsylvania Mental Health, Inc., Philadelphia, 1960.

Meyer, Carol. *Staff Development in Public Welfare Agencies*. New York: Columbia University Press, 1966.

Milbank Memorial Fund. *Programs for Community Mental Health*. Columbia University School of Social Work Library, 1957.

—— "Progress and Problems of Community Mental Health." 1959.

—— "Decentralization of Psychiatric Services and Continuity of Care," 1962.

National Association for Mental Health. *Technical Personnel in Mental Health.* New York, 1967.

National Study Service. Use of Volunteers in Public Welfare. Family Service Association of America. New York: 1963.

Orhansky, Mollie. "Children of the Poor." *Social Security Bulletin,* Vol. 26, July 1963, pp. 3-13.

Parad, H. J. *Crisis Intervention: Selected Readings.* New York: Family Service Association of America, 1965.

———— "Preventive Casework: Problems and Implications." In *Social Welfare Forum, National Conference on Social Welfare,* Columbia University Press, 1961, pp. 178-93.

Parad, H. J., and G. Caplan. "A Framework for Studying Families in Crisis." *Social Work,* 1960, pp. 5-15.

Pearl, A., and F. Reissman. *New Careers for the poor.* New York: Free Press, 1965.

Phelan, Joseph F., Jr. "Developing New Professional Categories of Volunteers in Child Welfare Services." *Child Welfare,* Vol. XLV, No. 4, April, 1966, pp. 214-17.

"President Endorses Social Work Manpower Need." Washington Memorandum. Washington: National Association of Social Workers, 1966, p. 1.

"Professions, The," *Daedalus: Journal of the American Academy of Arts and Sciences,* 1964.

Proposal for the Prevention and Control of Delinquency by Expanding Opportunities. New York: Mobilization for Youth, 1961.

Provence, Sally, and Rose Lipton. *Infants in Institutions.* New York: International Universities Press, 1962.

Psychiatric News. American Psychiatric Association, Washington, D.C., 1966-1968.

Psychiatric Spectator, Sandoz Pharmaceuticals, Hanover, New Jersey.

Public Health Concepts in Social Work Education: Proceedings of a seminar on public health concepts for social work schools. Council on Social Work Education, Princeton University, 1962.

Rae-Grant, Q. A., T. Gladwin, and E. Bower. "Mental Health, Social

Competence and the War on Poverty." *American Journal of Orthopsychiatry*, Vol. 36, No. 4, 1966.

Rapoport, L. "The Concept of Prevention in Social Work." *Social Work*, Vol. 6, 1:11, 1961.

——— "Working with Families in Crisis; An Exploration in Preventive Intervention." *Social Work*, Vol. 7, 3:48-56, 1962.

Reid, D. D. *Epidemiological Methods in the Study of Mental Disorders*. Public Health Paper No. 2, World Health Organization. Geneva, 1960.

Reiff, Robert. *Mental Health Manpower and Institutional Change*. Paper presented at University of Rochester Conference on Emergent Approaches to Mental Health Programs, 1955.

Reiff, R., and Frank Riessman. "The Indigenous Non-Professional: A Strategy of Change in Community Action and Community Mental Health Programs." *Community Mental Health Journal*, Monograph No. 1, 1965.

Rein, M., and R. Morris. "Goals, Structures and Strategies for Community Change." In *Social Work Practice*. National Conference Social Welfare. New York: Columbia University Press, 1962.

Riessman, Frank. *New Approaches to Mental Health Treatment for Labor and Low Income Groups*. National Institute of Labor Education. Mental Health Programs, New York, 1964.

——— "The 'helper' therapy principle." *Social Work*, 1965, Vol. 10, 27-32.

Riessman, Frank, et al. *Mental Health of the Poor*. New York: Free Press of Glencoe, 1964.

——— *The Culturally Deprived Child*. New York: Harper and Row, 1962.

Report of the National Advisory Commission on Civil Disorders. New York: Bantam Books, March 1968.

Richmond, Mary. *Friendly Visiting Among the Poor*. New York: Macmillan, 1899.

Rice, E. "Social Work in Public Health." *Social Work*, Vol. 4, 1:82-88, Jan. 1959.

Richan, W. "Theoretical Scheme for Determining Roles of Professional and Non-Professional Personnel." *Social Work*, Vol. 4, No. 4, Oct. 1961, pp. 22-28.

———— *Utilization of Personnel in Social Work: Those with Full Professional Education and Those Without.* Final Report of Sub-Committee on Utilization of Personnel, N.A.S.W. Commission on Practice, New York: mimeo, 1962.

Rioch, M., C. Elkes, and A. A. Flint. *Pilot Project in Training Mental Health Counselors.* Washington, D.C., National Institute of Mental Health, 1965. Public Health Service Publication # 1254.

Rothman, J. "An Analysis of Goals and Roles in Community Organization Practice." *Social Work*, 9:24-31, April 1964.

Sanders, I. T. *The Community.* New York: Ronald Press, 1958.

Sanders, R. *New Manpower For Mental Hospital Service.* Paper presented at University of Rochester Conference on Emergent Approaches to Mental Health Problems, University of Rochester, June, 1965.

Schmais, Aaron. *Implementing Non-Professional Programs in Human Services.* Manpower Training Series. New York: Center for the Study of Unemployed Youth, New York University, 1967.

Seyle, H. *The Stress of Life.* New York: McGraw-Hill, 1956.

Sieder, Violet M. "The Tasks of the Community Organization Worker." In *Planning Social Services for Urban Needs*, Columbia University Press, 1957.

Siegel, Seymour. *Nonparametric Statistics for the Behavioral Sciences.* New York: McGraw-Hill, 1956.

Sobey, Francine Sandell. A Study of the Problem of Homeless Well Babies Hospitalized at the N.Y. Infirmary. United Hospital Fund Research Study. Unpublished paper, 1959.

Stanton, A. H., and M. S. Schwartz. *The Mental Hospital.* New York: Basic Books, 1954.

Stead, Eugene, Jr. "Conserving Costly Talents—Providing Physicians' Assistant." *Journal of the American Medical Association*, Vol. 198, No. 10, Dec. 1966, pp. 182-83.

U. S. Bureau of the Census. U.S. Census of Population: 1950 &

1960. Vols. I & II. Characteristics of the Population. U.S. Government Printing Office, Washington, D.C., 1952 and 1963. Also Special Reports on Puerto Ricans in Continental United States, and Employment Status.

U. S. Congress. Mental Retardation Facility and Community Mental Health Centers Construction Act. Public Law 88-164, 88th Congress, Oct. 31, 1963.

U. S. Department of Health, Education and Welfare, Public Health Service. *The Comprehensive Community Mental Health Center: Concept and Challenge,* Publication No. 1137, April 1964.

——— Patient Movement Data, State and County Mental Hospitals, 1962. Public Health Service Public. No. 1282, The Model Reporting Area for Mental Health Hospital Statistics, 1964.

——— Mental Health Manpower: Current Statistical and Activities Report, Washington. Public Health Service, Vol. I, No. 1, 1964.

——— National Institute of Mental Health. Mental Health Statistics, Current Facility Reports, Published by National Clearinghouse for Mental Health Information, Chevy Chase, Md., Series MHB 1-11, MHBJ-1 Jan. 66-67.

——— Report of a Personnel Research Project. Public Health Service, Oct. 1964.

——— Towards Quality in Nursing: Needs and Goals. Public Health Service, No. 992, Feb. 1963.

——— The Psychiatric Aide in State Mental Hospitals. Public Health Service Publication No. 1286, March 1965.

——— Closing the Gap in Social Work Manpower, Nov. 1965.

——— Careers in Mental Health: Psychiatry, Psychiatric Social Work, Psychiatric Nursing and Clinical Psychology. Public Health Service, No. 23, 1960.

——— Pros and Cons: New Role for Non-Professionals in Corrections, by J. Benjamin, M. Freedman and E. Lynton, Office of Juvenile Delinquency and Youth Development. U.S. Government Printing Office, 1966.

——— Public Health Service, N.I.M.H. Community Mental Health

230

Centers Staffing Branch. Annotated bibliography on In-Service Training for Allied Professionals and Non-Professionals in Community Mental Health, 1968.

────── Utilization of Auxiliary Staff in the Provision of Family Services in Public Welfare, 1965.

U. S. Department of Labor. Manpower Research Bulletin No. 14, Technology and Manpower in the Health Service Industry, May 1967.

────── Manpower Report of the President—A Report on Manpower Requirements, Resources, Utilization and Training, March 1965.

────── The Manpower Act of 1965, Office of Manpower, Automation, and Training, Reprint No. 7, May 1965.

United States House of Representatives # 3688, 88th Congress, First Session, 1963. A Bill to provide for assistance in the construction and initial operation of community mental health centers and for other purposes.

United States Public Health Service. Planning of Facilities for Mental Health Services, Public Health Service, Publication No. 808, Washington, D.C. U.S. Government Printing Office, 1961.

The Wall Street Journal. Employ Varied Tactics to Ease Severe Nurse Shortage, Vol. 72, No. 5, Jan. 1965.

Weed, Vern, and William Denham. "Towards more Effective Use of the Nonprofessional Worker: A Recent Experiment." *Social Work,* Oct. 1961.

Wilensky, H. L., and C. N. Lebeaux. *Industrial Society and Social Welfare.* New York: Russell Sage Foundation, 1958.

Wittman, M. "Preventive Social Work: A Goal for Practice and Education." *Social Work,* Vol. 6, *1*:19-28, Jan. 1961.

────── Utilization of Personnel with Various Levels of Training: Implications of Professional Development. Paper presented at National Association of Social Workers, 10th Anniversary Symposium, Atlantic City, N. J. (May 22, 1965)

Yarrow, L. J. "Maternal Deprivation: Towards an Empirical and Conceptual Reevaluation." *Psychological Bulletin,* 58:459-90, 1961.

INDEX

Adolescents: service to, 57-60, 64; as nonprofessional workers, 80-84, 181

Advocate, 23

Aged: crisis of, 1, 20, 21, 59; as manpower resource, 4; service to the, 57-61, 61T, 83, 180; as nonprofessional workers, 80, 82, 84-86

Aide, in mental hospital, 28, 38; training of, 48; in rehabilitation, 41, 42; research findings on, 74-96, 76T, 78, 79T, 81T, 87T, 91T

Albee, George, 109

Alcoholics, service to, 1, 56, 58T, 59, 60, 60T, 61T, 62T, 63T, 64, 66, 67T, 116

Alienation, in modern society, 2, 25, 177; use of volunteers to combat, 25

Allied Health Manpower, 5

American Public Health Association, 3

Assessment, of nonprofessional contribution, 153-75

Barker, Robert L., 40, 43

Blain, Daniel, 17

Briggs, Thomas, 40, 43

Bureaucracies, effect on mental health, 1; use of volunteers in, 25

California Department of Mental Hygiene, 17

Caplan, Gerald, quoted, 7, 31

Career ladders, 5

Case aide, *see* Nonprofessional, job titles studied, 74-96

Chemotherapy, effect in changing treatment of mental hospital patients, 3, 17, 27

Citizen participation, 24, 46T

Civil Rights, 21

Civil Service, 84, 172, 173

Clergymen, 12, 18, 20

College students, 11, 15, 28, 57, 58T

Community action, 15

Community: hazards in, 2; citizen care in, 2, 3, 169, 176, 177, 178;

Community (*Cont.*)

comprehensive plans for the, 8; funds for treatment in the, 9; promoting mental health in the, 9, 29-33; early detection of mental disorder in the, 33-34; use of mental health principles in, 10; service goals to, 35; treatment of mentally ill in the, 27; nebulous concept of, 39, 43; outreach care in the, 56; volunteers as links to, 159, 160

Community mental health, *see* Mental health; *see also* Community, promoting mental health in the

Community mental health aide, 25, 29, 55, 74-96

Community mental health center, clinic, 10, 33, 34, 46T, 47, 49

Community Mental Health Centers Act (1963), 11, 31, 50

Community organizer, 33, *see* Nonprofessional, job titles studied, 74-96

Community out-reach care, 56, 65, 65T

Community psychiatry, 26

Core professionals in mental health, 2, 3, 176, 184

Correctional settings, 17; use of nonprofessionals, 23-24, 46T, 167

Counseling, 3, 4, 7, 23, 24, 31

Crime, in America, 1

Crisis, in America's mental health: nature of, 1-4, 12, 15, 45, 186; implications for manpower re-

sulting from, 3, 4, 6-12, 15; services needed in, 31-33; theories, 31

Custodial care, 11

Day care, 7, 30

Day hospital, *see* Community outreach care

Delinquents: service to, 56, 58, 59, 60, 61, 62, 63, 58T, 60T, 61T, 62T, 63T, 65T, 67T; as manpower, 93, 94

Drug addiction, 1, 185

Drug addicts: service to, 58T, 60T, 61T, 62T, 63, 63T, 66, 67T, 69, 167; as manpower resource, 90, 167

Dubos, René, 32

Education: of populations served by NIMH, 61-62, 62T; of nonprofessionals, 74, 86-90, 87T; of nonprofessionals and professionals, 183-185; *see also* Training, Mental health education, Educational services

Educational services, 4, 20, 21

Employment: career-entry in health, education and welfare, 5; in the human-services fields, 11, 20, 167, 181; as major goal in nonprofessional usage, 35; of hospital patients after discharge, 49; of indigenous nonprofessionals, 167; of practical nurses, 169

Enabler, 23

Environment, 1, 2, 12

Ethnic composition: of patients

served in NIMH projects, 62-63, 63T; of nonprofessional staff, 74, 90-95, 91T

Evaluation: of large-scale nonprofessional job programs, 5; *see also* Assessment of nonprofessional contribution

Expeditor, 11, 23, 90

Erikson, Eric, 31

Family agencies, 1

Federal Community Mental Health Centers Act (1963), *see* Community Mental Health Center Act

Financial aid, 7

Finestone, Samuel, 39, 41

Foster Care, 4, 11, 65T, 67T

Freud, Sigmund, 2, 141

Funding, for prevention, 29

Greenfield, Harry, 5

Group counseling, 23; *see also* Counseling

Halfway house, *see* Community out-reach care

Health Professionals Educational Assistance Act of 1963, 20

Health professions, 20

Health services, 20

Heyman, Margaret, 39, 41

Hollingshead and Redlich, studies by, 18

Home Care, 11; *see also* Community out-reach care

Hospital, *see* Inpatient care, Hospital Improvement Grant Program, Mental illness, treatment in hospital

Hospital Improvement Grant Program, Mental illness, treatment

Housewives, manpower potential of, 4, 11

Housing, 7, 21

Human services, employment in, 11; for new manpower groups, 11

Indigenous nonprofessional; 5, 11, 21, 33, 68, 74, 93-95, 115, 151, 152, 160, 167, 172, 181, 183, 187

Infancy, 2

Innovation; in manpower usage, 10-12, 19; defined, 11, 148; in nonprofessional titles, 55; in types of care given, 56, 65-69; in groups served, 59; index devised, 72, 148-149; research in, 185

Inpatient care, 57, 65T, 67T, 71

James, George, 3

Job titles, nonprofessional: research findings on, 74-96, 76T, 78T, 81T, 87T, 91T

Joint Commission on Mental Illness and Health, 9, 31, 127

Labor unions: mental health care plans in, 3; mental health nonprofessionals working in, 47; related to "New Careers," 38

Levine, Eugene, 39, 41

Lewin, Kurt, 152

Liaison aide, 23

Lincoln Hospital Mental Health Service Program, 36

Lindemann, Eric, 31

Manpower: health, 5, 17

Manpower, mental health: quantity, type needed for mental health, illness, 1-4; shortage of nonprofessionals in, 2, 21; ratio of professionals to nonprofessionals, 3, 53-54, 70, 71; potential of new resources, 4, 11; goals in prevention and treatment, 6, 26-34; concepts and broad trends in use of, 17-43; related to economic and social policy, 19-25; changing allocations, 39-43; changing work models for, 40-43; *see also* Nonprofessionals, Professional staff, Volunteer, nonprofessional and professional, Indigenous nonprofessional

Medical, 8, 16, 17, 22

Medical Tribune and Medical News, 17

Medicare, 3

Mental disorder, 6, 7; *see also* Mental illness

Mental health: environment conducive to, 2; crisis in, 1-4, 12, 15, 45; services, 3, 18, 21, 25, 27, 28, 39, 45-69; limited study of, 7; principles of, 10; scope of the term, 12; goals of, 13, 122-49; changing planning base in, 10; in the family, 31

Mental Health Education, 7, 25

Mental health project, defined in survey, 45; types of projects, 45-47; location of project by agency setting and grant program auspices, 46T; auspices of, 47-48, 48T; in different types of agencies, 49-50

Mental health programs, *see* Mental health (services); Mental illness (expanding programs)

Mental illness: estimate of extent in United States, 1; treatment in hospital and community, 2, 9, 27-33, 56-71; manpower needed for treatment of, 2, 3; changing demands for treatment of, 2, 3, 45; expanding programs and services, 3; historical view of, 9

Minority groups: mental health manpower potential in, 4; untouched by professional mental health services, 18; problems of, 20-45; employment of, 21

Mobilization for Youth, 36, 83

Mount Sinai School of Medicine, 3

National Assembly on Mental Health Education, 25

National Commission on the Causes and Prevention of Violence, 7

National Institute of Mental Health: research sponsored by, 13; overview of Project Study, 44

Neighborhood agent, 23

Neighborhood aide, 25

Neighborhood centers, 3

Neighborhood Service Centers, 37, 167, 176

New Careers, 5, 37, 38, 166

New York City Community Mental Health Board, 27

New York City Department of Social Services, 40

Nonprofessionals: need for study of, 4-6; in New Careers, 5, 37, 38; as new and traditional manpower, 10, 11, 55; as expedient resource, 11; defined, 12; organization of survey data on, 12-14; as public mental hospital personnel, 18; in treatment of the mentally ill, 26-29, 70, 171, 177; in promotion of community mental health, 29-33, 70; in early detection of mental disorder, 33-34, 70; work milieu of 44-54; history of prior use of, 50, 55; data on characteristics, 73-96; job titles studied, 74-96, 76T, 78T, 81T, 87T, 91T, 102; sex, age, paid vs. volunteer status studied, 74-86, 79T, 81T; education, ethnicity, and indigeneity studied, 86-95, 87T, 91T; functions performed, 97-108, 177; in prevention, 124, 126, 128, 131-35, 138-49; see also Indigenous nonprofessional, Manpower, Mental health

Nurses, 2, 20, 177, 168, 184

Nursing, 16, 17, 41, 43, 55, 76T, 79T, 81T, 87T, 91T, 110, 176, 193

Occupational therapy, 41

O.E.O., p. 14, 15

Paraprofessional, 12

Personnel, mental health, see manpower, mental health, also professional, nonprofessional volunteer, preventive mental health personnel

Physical therapy, 41

Planned parenthood aides, 9, 10

Planning, mental health: governmental and nongovernmental, 5, 20; in formulation of Manpower policy, 7, 20, 21; changes in, 10; for mental health goals, 13; Study of California Department of Mental Hygiene, 17; for the ill and needy, 29; implications, 181

Population changes, in relation to changing demand for treatment, 3, 4

Poverty: related to mental illness, 1, 22; changes in concept of, 21-24; models of care for, 22-23; nonprofessional responsibility for problems of, 22, 23; target of NIMH projects
target of NIMH projects

Preventive index: 45, 71, 140-147, 143T, 145T, 146T, 149, 180, 185

Preventive intervention: manpower needed for, 4, 6, 7; public health classification of levels, 6, 7, 185; lack of study of, 7; coordinated with comprehensive community

Preventive intervention (*Cont.*)
  planning, 8; nonprofessional usage in, 8, 124-49; *see also* Planning, Mental health
Preventive mental health, personnel, 10, 32
Preventive mental health services, 4, 7, 29
Primary prevention: defined, 6, 7; examples of services in, 7, 122, 180; handicaps to, 30; nonprofessional usage in, 29-33, 70; differentiated from other levels, 123; neglect of, 125; study and analysis of goals of, 124-37, 127T, 129T, 136T, 137T, 139; nonprofessional contribution to, 158
Professional staff: in mental health, 3, 4, 39, 121; nonmental health, 20; functions compared with nonprofessional, 103-106, 104T; interaction with nonprofessionals, 161-65, 161T; distinct from nonprofessional, 173-74; *see also* Manpower, Mental health
Professions, formal training requirement, 12; historical changes in the, 16-18; standard-setting by the, 36, 37; status and power issues in the, 34-39
Public health, 7, 8, 46T
Psychiatric aide, *see* Aide, in mental hospital
Psychiatrists, 2, 18, 54, 184
Psychiatry: manpower problems in, 17, 18; knowledge pursued in, 16; recruitment needed in, 110
Psychologists, 3, 41, 51, 184

Psychology, 16, 176
Psychotherapy, 3, 27
Public services, 21
Public welfare, 17, 25, 40, 160

Race, relations, 1
Ratios, of nonprofessionals to professionals, 3; of professionals in public mental hospitals, 17
Ratios, of professionals to nonprofessionals, 3, 53-54, 70, 71, 179; in community vs. institutional settings, 70, 71, 187; in projects of over 100 nonprofessionals, 95-96
Reach-out aide, 23, 156, 178
Recreation, group-work aide, *see* Nonprofessionals, job titles studied
Recruitment, 28, 109-19, 189; methods used, 111-12, 113; problems in, 113-15; of special groups, 115-17
Rehabilitation aide, *see* Aide, in rehabilitation
Reiff, Robert, 30
Research: related to large-scale nonprofessional job programs, 5; dearth of in manpower utilization, 5; little available on prevention, 7; based on preventive levels in this, 7; help in planning, 9; findings from NIMH survey, 13
Retired persons, potential of, 11, 181
Richmond, Mary, 24
Riessman, Frank, 5, 23, 38
Rusk, Howard A., quoted, 10, 41

Salaries, comparative in different fields, 20

School drop-outs, 10, 11, 57, 58T, 60T, 61T, 62T, 63T, 83, 84, 169, 180

Screening, for mental health service; 100, 101T, 104T; of nonprofessional staff, 112-13, 178

Secondary prevention; defined, 6, 123; neglect of, 181; study and analysis of goals of, 124-37, 127T, 129T, 136T, 137T, 139; nonprofessional contribution to, 158

Self-help, 23, 83, 152, 167

Services, see Mental health, Mental illness, Crisis, also Preventive mental health services, Educational services, Health services

Site-visit interview, 13

Social change, 2, 19

Social disorder, 6, 7

Social inequality, effect on mental health, 1

Social isolation, 24, 26

Social rehabilitation, of the mentally ill, 3, 180

Social therapies, 3

Social work, 16, 17, 23, 40, 42, 43, 110, 176, 193

Social workers, 2, 20, 22, 40, 42, 43, 54, 184

Storefront center, see Community out-reach care

Subprofessional, 12

Supervision, of nonprofessionals, 18, 109, 120-21, 153, 154, 155, 161T, 162, 171, 193

Survey, as tool for book's findings, 13-15

Teachers, 18, 20; as aides, 76-96

Tertiary prevention: defined, 6, 123; study and analysis of goals of, 124-40, 127T, 129T, 136T, 137T; nonprofessional contribution to, 157, 174

Topeka State Hospital, 38

Training: for the health professions, 20; in corrections, 24; personnel to care for mentally ill, 28, 169; needed for secondary prevention goals, 34; of nonprofessional groups, 109, 117-20, 178, 182; expense of, 153, 154, 155, 161T; changes in, 171, 174

United States Census Bureau of the Budget, 50

Vocational guidance, 3

Volunteer nonprofessional: facts of usage of, 5; defined, 12; activities in mental health, 25-26; in public welfare, 25, 159; history of use in mental hospitals, 50; work pattern, 52; in recreation and group work, 78-79; recommendations for, 183; potential of, 193; see also Manpower, Mental health

Volunteer professional, 12

Wage scales, 28

Youth: problems of, 1, 2, 20; as mental health manpower potential, 4